Teaching Film Animation to Children

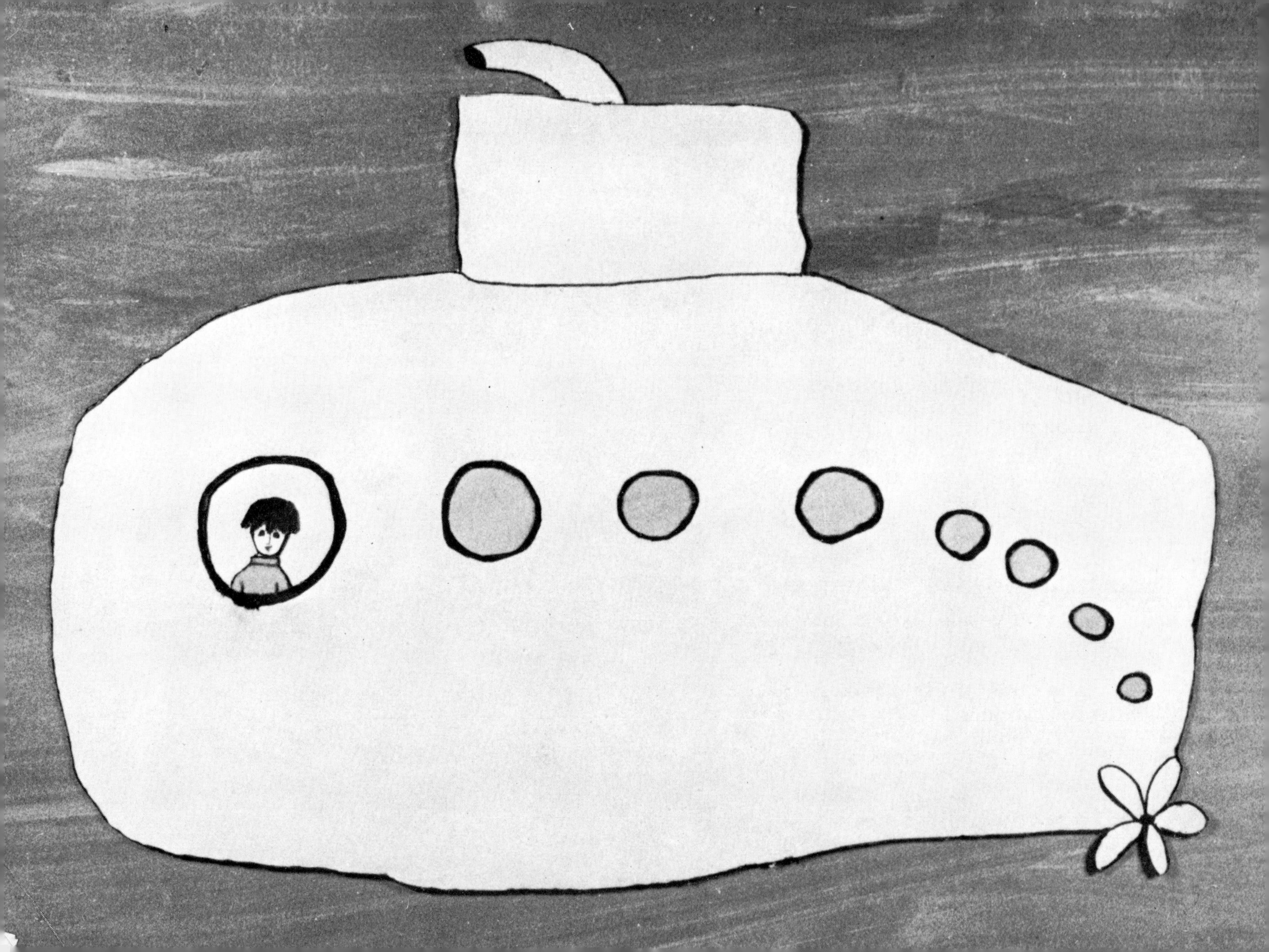

Teaching Film Animation to Children

Yvonne Andersen

VAN NOSTRAND REINHOLD COMPANY
NEW YORK CINCINNATI TORONTO LONDON MELBOURNE

Van Nostrand Reinhold Company Regional Offices:
New York Cincinnati Chicago Millbrae Dallas
Van Nostrand Reinhold Company Foreign Offices:
London Toronto Melbourne

Library of Congress Catalog Card Number 72-126985

Printed by Halliday Lithograph Corporation
Color printed by Bridge Litho Co., Inc.
Bound by Complete Books Company

Published by Van Nostrand Reinhold Company
450 West 33rd Street, New York, N.Y. 10001
Published simultaneously in Canada by Van Nostrand Reinhold Company Ltd.

16 15 14 13 12 11 10 9 8 7 6 5 4 3 2 1

Acknowledgments:

Dominic Falcone, my husband, and our children, Jean and Paul Falcone;

My film students at The Yellow Ball Workshop, Projects Inc., Cellar Door Cinema, and Newton Creative Arts Center;

My assistants at these schools: Dominic Falcone, Susan Gittleman, Mary Austin, Marjorie Lenk, Joanne Ricca, Elizabeth Archer, Carol Sones;

And Albert Hurwitz, Coordinator of the Arts, Newton Public Schools; Marjorie Lenk, Director, Lexington School of Modern Dance (Cellar Door Cinema); Rita DeLisi, Director, Projects Inc.; Rev. John S. Culkin, Director, Center for Understanding Media; Dr. Gerald O'Grady, Director, Media Center, University of St. Thomas; Anthony Hodgkinson, Boston University Film Department; Harris Cohen and staff of Back Bay Film Laboratory; The DePhoure family of D-4 Film Laboratory; Alvin Fiering, President, Polymorph Films Inc.; Bernt Pettersen, President, Envision Corporation.

Photographs Yvonne Andersen, Dominic Falcone, Joanne Ricca

Contents

Preface

The philosophy of this book is that film animation is basically the bringing to life of paintings and sculptures. Animated cinema gives children and adults alike the exciting ability to create a dynamic world of moving, speaking creatures by using simple art supplies and a camera. It is a new way of exploring one's ingenuity and a new mode of communication as well as of self-expression.

Rather than dealing with the traditional methods of filming cartoon strips, the author concentrates on fresh ways to unite camera and art work. This unique medium of expression is especially suited to children because it arouses their imagination. It is dynamic enough to stimulate them and yet easy enough for them to handle.

This approach to film animation evolved from the author's years of teaching experience at several schools, particularly at the Yellow Ball Workshop, which the author created and still directs. The workshop opened in the fall of 1963 as a Saturday art class for children. Film animation was introduced as one of the many experiments in art media, but it quickly grew in popularity and now is the total concern of the workshop and its staff.

Workshop courses in film animation include the creation of art work; the handling of the camera and of sound and editing equipment; and the preparation of the story. These courses are open to students varying in age from 6 to 18, and also to adult students and teachers. It was at the workshop that teachers and students, working together, developed new techniques in animation to help the young artist to be more creative while doing less of the repetitive tasks formerly required for animation.

The workshop arrangement is ideal not only for schoolchildren or adults engaged in educational programs but also for groups of all sorts. For instance, clubs and associations seeking to broaden their interests might take up film animation as a group project. And the techniques described are as suitable for individual study as for group study. So, while it might not be feasible for every group or individual to emulate *all* aspects of the workshop setup, it is important to know how the workshop operates.

The aim of this book is to guide any adult who desires to teach film animation. Toward that goal, the book describes how a workshop is organized so that time and equipment are put to the best use.

The workshop provides equipment, film, and art supplies; the staff members provide encouragement and, together with their students, they explore the answers to aesthetic and technical questions. The atmosphere is not like a classroom, but more like a gathering place, where participants are free to create new worlds in the expressive medium of film. Anything is possible in animation.

Simple techniques are used by beginning students, while advanced students develop more complex techniques. The book deals first with cutout animation because it involves less work and expense than some of the other techniques and yet is still dramatically expressive. The later chapters go on to explain other types of animation and the entire topic of sound techniques. There are also special instructions on how to adapt inexpensive cameras for use in animation though they may not have all of the devices necessary.

Animated films made by the workshop students at Yellow Ball and other schools have won prizes in international film festivals, have been shown on nationwide television, and are in the collections of schools and libraries in the United States, Canada, and Europe. Some of these films are available for rental. They are for sale only to educational institutions. To obtain a brochure on these films, write to the Yellow Ball Workshop; 62 Tarbell Avenue; Lexington, Massachusetts, 02173.

The representative films described and pictured in this book were done in the years from 1965 to 1969 by students who were 6 to 17 years old and who were at different stages in their development during this time. Therefore, the age given for each student corresponds to the year in which he or she worked on the particular film described.

Film animation is the bringing to life of art work by means of a motion picture camera. The techniques described in this book eliminate many of the repetitive tasks needed for traditional cartoon animation. Mark Mahoney, 12, cuts out a painted form for his animated film Charlie and His Harley. ▶

What Is a Film?

If you examine a strip of movie film, you will see that it consists of a series of still pictures in a vertical row, each one just a little different from the one which preceded it. This is true in both live-action film and in animated film. Let us take the example of a scene which lasts for one second and in which a live actor lifts an apple from a table and takes a bite. The camera would record this as 24 separate still pictures, called frames, showing the action in various stages. When the film is run through a projector, we see the different stages so quickly that they appear as continuous movement.

In animation we produce action by filming the art work one or two frames at a time, and then moving the character a little before taking the next frame. In the illustrated example from *Cinder City,* the character "Smirk" (created by Peter Bull, 11) smokes a cigarette. The smoke puffs out of the end of the cigarette, each cloud getting bigger and bigger. As the smoke floats upward, the clouds become smaller, until they disappear. For the sake of space, each photograph on page 14 in which smoke appears represents two frames of film. The head and background were painted onto a piece of background paper. The puffs of smoke and the cigarette are separate paper cutouts, and the smoke cutouts are changed each time the cameraman has taken two frames of the preceding cutout.

In a close-up facial scene, such as the one of "Smirk," the camera operator begins by taking 24 frames of the face with nothing moving. (The opposite photo represents all 24 frames.) This one second of film is long enough for the picture to register on the audience. Then the movable parts are animated for at

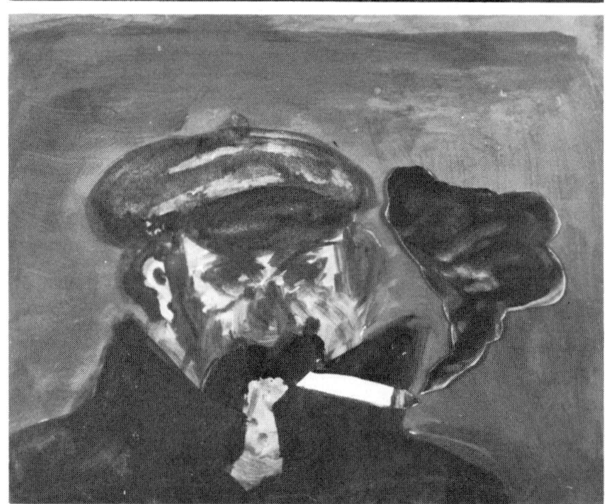
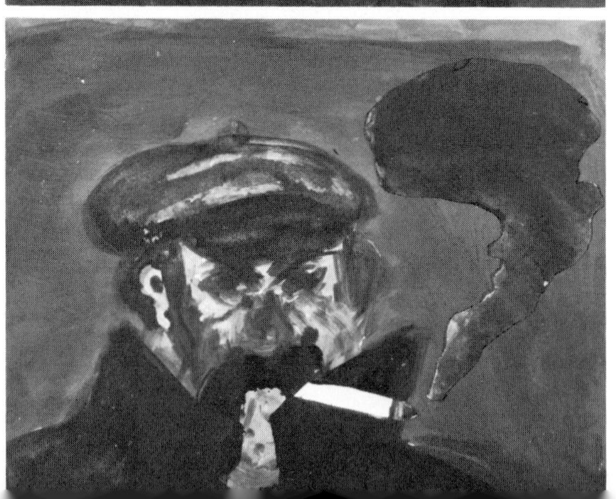

least 24 frames, changing them after every 2 frames. Finally, the face is filmed with nothing moving for 24 frames. This results in a filmed scene that lasts for three seconds. (The five photographs with smoke show only 10 of the animated frames. The other 14 frames would repeat the sequence of smoke puffs growing larger and floating away before the final 24 frames of the face were filmed.)

These examples show that both live-action and animated films are a series of separate, still pictures. In both cases, the camera's mechanism moves the film forward so that each frame is exposed individually. However, in live-action work, the camera's trigger is used to activate the mechanism, and the film moves forward at a constant speed, measured in frames per second. (Remember that in the apple-biting scene 24 frames resulted in one second of film. This rate of 24 frames per second is the normal shooting speed for 8mm and 16mm cameras when sound is to be added.) Animation does not use the constant-speed method of filming.

In animation, a device called a single-frame release is used to activate the camera. The single frame is exposed and the film is automatically advanced one frame for the next exposure. The shooting speed of the camera is irrelevant because the separate frames are taken at whatever time intervals you choose instead of at a constant rate. Nevertheless, you shoot 24 frames in order to obtain one second of film because the movie projector also runs at a constant rate of speed—in the case of an 8mm or 16mm sound projector, 24 frames per second.

◀ *A film is a series of still pictures that give the illusion of continuous motion. The character "Smirk," by Peter Bull, 11, appears to smoke a cigarette merely because the size and position of the puffs of smoke are changed after every two pictures. This is the basis of animation, and the simplest way to accomplish the necessary changes is by using movable cutouts on a painted background.*

Whether the film is a live-action one or an animated one, when it is run through a projector, the separate frames follow each other at a constant, rapid speed, giving the illusion of continuous motion.

These paper cutouts of smoke puffs and a cigarette are placed on the portrait of "Smirk" and filmed so that the puffs grow larger, then decrease and float away.
▼

Supplies and Work Space

Motion Picture Equipment

The first requirement is a movie camera. It can be either 8mm, Super 8mm or 16mm. The 8mm and Super 8mm cameras are inexpensive, with prices starting at about $25. The cost of a 50-foot roll of color film, which is about four minutes long, is about $5, complete with processing. Super 8mm is recommended if the class is to experiment with animation but will film mostly live action, or if all the students are very young, or if the class needs as many cameras as possible.

It is very useful in animation to have a camera which can take single frames, and which has reflex viewing and focusing. (The image coming through the lens is reflected by mirrors to the viewfinder, which incorporates a ground glass—or some other method of determining the image's sharpness—to guide you as you adjust the lens. The reflex camera shows you exactly what the lens sees.) If your camera does not have these capabilities, certain problems will arise. As explained in the last chapter, you can solve these problems, but it will require extra time and effort.

Some 8mm and Super 8mm cameras have these three features. The ones that do usually cost $150 and up. It would be possible to purchase the camera plus inexpensive Super 8mm equipment for animation for about $400. The following list gives each item and its approximate price.

Camera (new)	$150
Light meter (new)	20
Two light stands (new)	40
Editing set (new)	40
Projector (new)	100
Tripod (new)	50

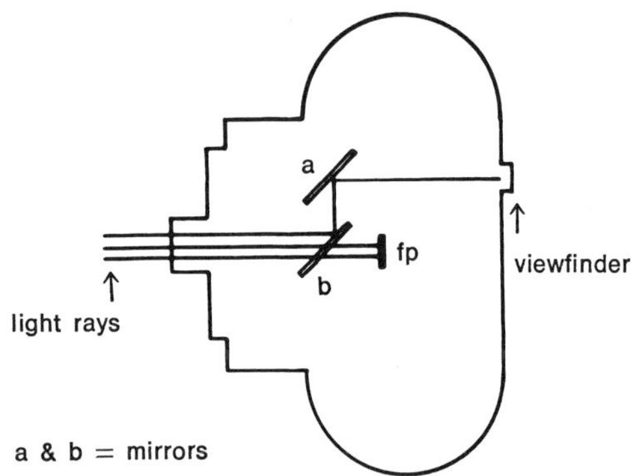

◀ *The basic mechanics of a reflex viewer are simple. The light rays entering the lens hit a mirror and are deflected to another mirror, which transmits them to a viewfinder. In a partially-silvered mirror—as at left—only a part of the light is deflected, giving a dim image. The rest hits the film plane (**fp**) when the camera is in operation. For reflex focusing, a ground glass or other device is incorporated in the viewfinder. Reflex cameras with a rotating mirror allow more light to be deflected for viewing and focusing, but they pose other problems.*

Basic equipment includes a movie camera mounted on a tripod. Here, Paul Shoul, 11, operates the camera, as all students are taught to do. ▶

A light meter measures the lighting conditions and indicates the correct combination of settings (frames per second and lens opening) for exposing the film. Try to get a meter that is marked in frames per second, not in shutter speeds for still cameras, though you can convert still shutter speeds to frames per second. The light stands (for photoflood lamps) and the tripod to hold the camera must be sturdy. The editing set, which includes a splicer, will be explained later.

The items listed are absolutely basic. However, if the total cost exceeds your budget, you can get secondhand equipment for much less money. It might even be possible, through much scouting around, to get completely outfitted for $100.

Our classes use a 16mm Bolex reflex camera for animation. We prefer this camera for several reasons. The picture it takes is sharper, brighter, and larger than an 8mm picture, and 16mm film can have an optical sound track added. Also, because 16mm sound projectors are standard equipment in many schools, churches, museums, theaters and libraries, the films can be shown almost anywhere.

A 16mm Bolex reflex camera with one wide-angle 10mm Switar lens can be bought new for around $750, and secondhand for about $400. Anyone working within a school system would probably not have to buy a projector, as the school usually has one. A good 16mm sound projector costs about $700. A good used one could be bought for about $250. If the camera is secondhand, and the school provides the projector, a 16mm outfit would cost about $550, itemized as follows:

Camera (secondhand)	$400
Projector (by the school)	00
Tripod (new)	50
Light meter (new)	20
Editing set (new)	40
Two light stands (new)	40

With this 16mm equipment, you can make very high quality films which can be shown on television as well as in schools. The high cost of 16mm film is minimized in animation, because you spend the most time on planning and making art work and less time shooting film. Our experience is that for every 200 feet you might shoot while working in live action, you would shoot 10 feet in animation. The cost of a 100-foot roll of 16mm color film lasting about three minutes is approximately $15, complete with processing. This estimate holds true only if you buy your film a dozen rolls at a time from a film lab or directly from Eastman Kodak. If you have a work print (copy of the original) made, the cost goes up to about $30.

Art Materials

Except for one type of paper, the art supplies necessary for animation are usually already available in most schools' art departments. This paper is two-ply, medium-finish bristol board, which comes in pads 11 inches by 14 inches. This paper is excellent for use in cutout animation because it does not curl up so much when painted, and it is thick and heavy enough so that hinged, cutout characters can withstand much handling. An inexpensive brand of this paper costs about $1.20 per pad of 20 sheets. While it is not absolutely necessary to use bristol board, the results are worth the added expense.

The other basic supplies are poster paints, brushes, Cray-Pas crayons (oil color in stick form), soft pencils, erasers, masking tape, thread, scissors, rubber cement, Elmer's Glue, soft, non-hardening clay (plasteline), sheets of white cardboard, felt-tipped pens, etc.

The Work Room

The main work room should be one used for art classes, so that it has running water to wash brushes and also has places to store art supplies. If this room always has a lot of outside light, and if there is a place near a window where you can set up your camera, you could also use this for filming. In that case, you would not need the light stands. You would just film with available light.

If the room used for art work does not have sufficient light and space for camera work, you can use a small, dark room or a sufficient-sized storage closet for actual filming. In the latter two instances, you would have to illuminate the art work with photoflood lamps instead of daylight. You can use either outside light or artificial light with color film, but not both at the same time.

Storage for Art Work

The proper storage of art work from one class session to the next is always a problem. One solution is to have each child keep his art work in a sturdy, red rope envelope. These may be stored collectively at the school or some other suitable place by the teacher, or each child may store his own envelope at home.

The red envelopes work very well for flat cutouts. However, art work for three-dimensional animation is more difficult to store. This would include either clay characters and sets (heavy and easily crushed) or papier-mâché characters and sets (large and bulky). Storage must be planned for in advance. For this reason, you should check out your working area very carefully before you plan your projects. Otherwise it may take far more time to set up the scenery and clean up afterwards than should be necessary.

One year, for example, when a class was being held in a room usually reserved for nursery-school children, we made pixillated films (animation using live actors) in which each student painted scenery 8 feet high and 10 feet wide. The scenery had to be taped up on the wall before the class arrived and taken down and rolled up afterwards. There were 12 such pieces of scenery. The students also had paper-bag masks and paper costumes. These were stored in suitcases. It was necessary to arrive two hours before this class was even scheduled to meet.

Not only did the scenery have to be put up, the room had to be cleared of nursery toys and small furniture beforehand. Then the heavy tables and chairs had to be dragged out for our class. Paper and canvas had to be laid down everywhere to protect tables, walls and floors. After the class was over, it took another two hours to clean the whole thing up. Just because we did not have the right kind of place to work in, the teacher had to spend four out of six hours in heavy labor instead of conducting a class.

Using an editor, Tristian Hickey, 12, views the film frame by frame. ▶ Editing film is one of the procedures every student learns.

Class Organization

Students

Workshop experience shows a class should have a maximum of 12 students with two instructors. It is possible to have only one instructor if all the work is done in the same room. A class could have more students if they worked together on a group project rather than each one making a separate film.

The student in a film production class has a lot of ground to cover. He learns how to operate a movie camera, light meter, projector, editor, tape recorder, and he also works on the story and the preparation of art work for filming. The fewer the students, the more film work each will have a chance to learn.

Since this is an animation class, the students should be persons strongly interested in drawing and painting. A student interested only in live-action filming, or a person who just wants to learn how to handle the equipment, should not be encouraged to enter this class. In a film animation class, there is nothing to film until the student has created some art work. If the study of animation is purely a group project, it is legitimate for the individual members to specialize—some creating the art work, and some maneuvering the camera.

Our workshops have had students as young as five years old, but we do not especially recommend it. We find that artistically talented young students can do beautiful art work, make good stories and animate their characters well. The things they cannot do well are: run the projector, operate a light meter and make splices (joints in film). Sometimes a very young child who learns how to make splices one year has to be taught the very same operation all over again the next year. Very young children do not retain technical information as well as 9- or 10-year-olds.

As a workshop, we have had classes of all 10-year-old boys, classes of all teen-agers and classes of all adults. We find that it is best to have mixed ages whenever possible. Even classes combining children and adults seem to work out well. If the students are all of a similar age, the eccentricities of that age are magnified. The 10-year-old boys will be happy and noisy, singing songs as they paint. The teen-agers will be very conversational and social and not get their work done in time. In a class of twelve, a good ratio is about six older teen-agers to about four youngsters of 10 to 13 years old, and no more than two students in the 8 to 10 age group. This is not always possible. If you can have a class like this, the older teen-agers will lend their discipline to the situation and the younger ones will liven it up

The Instructor and the Assistant

The instructor in a film animation class should have an art background or a strong interest in art. He should know how to operate the camera, projector, editor, and tape recorder. He should make a short animated film himself before teaching a class. If he does this, he will discover firsthand what some of the problems might be.

The assistant should also know how to operate the camera and be able to instruct children in this. In animation, it is useful to have the assistant in charge of filming. The instructor supervises the creation of art and story and editing. The assistant should be willing to get his hands dirty and help the instructor set up the materials and equipment and get the class cleaned up afterwards. A good assistant is a valuable asset, and allows the class to progress more smoothly than it could otherwise.

Class Hours

In the winter, the workshop holds classes for two hours once a week and during the summer for two hours every morning for five weeks. In all, a student attends about 50 hours of classes. This is usually enough time for a student to make a one-minute animated film. The length of the film is not the important factor. The quality of the film is. Some students have made wonderful 30-second films which tell a whole story in that length of time. Others need three or four minutes to complete an artistic unit.

Types of Film: The Importance of Fast Processing

Students are always eager to see the results of their first film-making venture and viewing the film generates enthusiasm. Therefore, the exposed film should be processed as soon as possible.

The workshop's first films were shot on Kodachrome II. We set up our camera near an open window and used daylight for filming. This film took four or five days to have processed and returned to us from the laboratory. It was then viewed and edited by the class.

In later years, when we were filming in a dark room, we used Ektachrome Commercial, a very beautiful film. This, too, took almost a week to have processed, and we also had the laboratory make a work print, or copy, of the film. That way we could store the original film and work with the copy.

The value of having a work print is that it does not matter if the students accidentally scratch it and tear it. They can use it to learn how to load a projector; to run it back and forth many times in making a sound track; and to edit it in the viewer, arranging the scenes by cutting the film and joining (splicing) the ends together. If they change their minds about placement of scenes, they can easily make new splices, joining the film in new positions. If the work film gets torn, you can have another copy made from the original without having to refilm the whole scene again.

At present, we use mainly Ektachrome EF. This is the film most used for television newscasts. We can get one-day service from our laboratory on this film. If we get the film to them by 9:00 A.M., they can process the original by noon and make a work print by 3:30 P.M. This fast service is available from film labs which do a lot of television work.

If we were to use Kodachrome II or Ektachrome Commercial, as we formerly did, we would have to wait four or five days to get the film back. This is a drawback when the class meets daily. It is essential to have your first roll of film back by the third lesson so that the class can see how it turned out. After that, you should try to have a roll back at least every third lesson. Having a viewing session is usually a great morale builder.

Philosophy

The film animation classes described here are extra-curricular. Some are held within the public school system, but most are held in private schools. Wherever the classes are held, the assumption is that there are no students in the class who do not want to be there. Each class is run as a workshop. It is a place where the individual artist goes to learn how to express himself through the medium of the animated film. The student learns operation of equipment. He is permitted to make any kind of story or other expression with this medium he wishes. There is no censorship. It is a grown-up place. The new student is guided along, one step at a time, in technique; but he is allowed to create any sort of story he wishes.

As teachers, we enjoy watching the creation of a personal-experience type of story, but the student can make a cowboy, or gangster or super-hero type of story if he prefers. We have noticed that girls often make personal stories, and boys make more violent stories. This is especially the case with children under the age of 13. As the student gets older, his films become more sophisticated and may deal with humor, irony, tragedy or social comment. The classic emotion in animation is humor, but we encourage the students to forget previous animated films they have seen and to think of animation as a means of making their drawings and paintings move and come to life.

The teacher's function is manifold. He provides art supplies, instructs in the use of equipment, answers questions, takes the film to the lab and schedules the filming and sound-track activities. But the teacher also gives moral support and encourages the student to make new discoveries by himself. These new discoveries are the element which makes the class a joy for the teacher and the student.

Jean Falcone, 8, paints some art work she will use in a film. ▶

JUICES LICKING
WHIPPING AROUND
THE RED THROUGH
POURS
INSIDE
Pamela

The First Lesson

There are two most important elements in teaching a film animation class. They are: (1) motivation of students, and (2) organization of facilities and procedures. Before our class actually starts making an animated film, we show the students a few very good finished films. This creates a climate of excitement and enthusiasm. Many students already have cinematic ideas and animation is a chance for them to tell a story in the compelling, dramatic medium of film.

The staff takes the students through the steps one at a time, never giving excess technical information before it can be absorbed. New students work with cutouts first. Cutouts are a good first project because they are not only simple, dramatic and inexpensive, but they can express any kind of movement.

To begin, each student needs only paper, paint, and scissors for the first project, which is to paint a large face that fills most of an 11-by-14-inch sheet of bristol board. Whatever is to move on this page should not be painted in. The movable part could be the mouth, eyes, eyebrows, or even hair. The head could be made to turn from side to side by alternating the front view with profile cutouts. A hand with a hot dog or a sandwich could move into the scene.

The part that is to move should be painted separately on another piece of paper and cut out. Painting the page and the cutouts is all that the students do in the first lesson. They do not even discuss the story yet.

For the first animation project, it is wise to have each child make only one movable feature on the face. If a student is very ambitious or experienced, another movable part can be added.

Painted portrait done for The Country Scene *by Andrea Dietrich, 11 at the time, uses different cutouts of the hair and mouth as the movable parts.*

The two space-ship travelers in The Atomic Robot, *by Paul Falcone, then 8, each has eyeballs that can shift and a mouth that opens and closes by using three cutouts.*

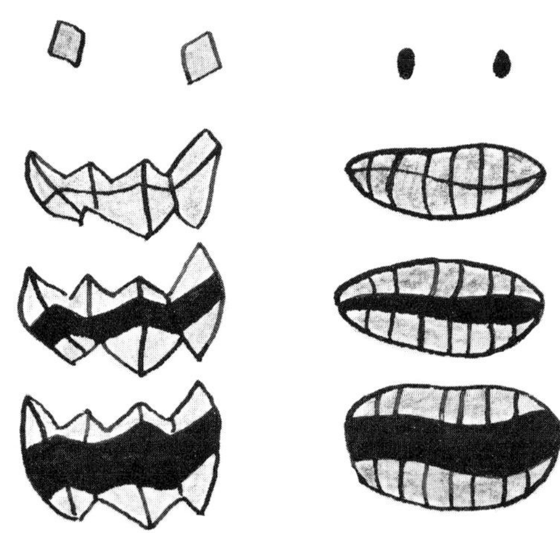

In a close-up from *The Country Scene,* by Andrea Dietrich, 11, the girl's hair blows in the wind, and she says, "I came all the way from the city in a bus, and I don't see any country animals." The movable parts are the hair and the mouth. They are changed every two frames. The cutout mouth is laid on top of the painted-in mouth, photographed for two frames, and then removed for two frames.

In *The Atomic Robot,* by Paul Falcone, 8, the space-ship creatures peer out of their porthole at the earth. One speaks in a robot-like voice. "I see a good place to land." The other says, "We will des-troy, des-troy, des-troy." The eyeballs of each creature roll from side to side and each one's mouth opens and closes.

A face moving from side to side can indicate the character is turning to look at something or is shaking its head to say no. This can be done even if the head is painted in along with the background. You merely make the side-view cutouts a little bigger than the front view, so that they will cover it when laid on top. There is no need to make intermediate views.

In a scene from *Eagle,* by Mimi Kravitz, 15, the eagle on a coin turns his head from side to side so the audience of admiring onlookers can see him from all sides. Because the bird's neck is smaller in profile than it is from the front, all three views had to be separate paintings.

Two side views and a front view allows this eagle by Mimi Kravitz, 15, to be filmed so it appears to turn its head from side to side.

Possible Problems

(1) The students should be told to keep the paper's long dimension horizontal when they paint the portraits for filming. This is because the camera takes an oblong picture. The horizontal part of the rectangle is bigger than the vertical part. If a vertical portrait is filmed, the camera will take in part of the supporting background (the table or floor) as well as the art work placed there. If a child paints a vertical portrait by mistake, the face can be cut out and mounted on a larger piece of paper so the final effect is horizontal. The camera will have to be moved farther away from the art work, but sometimes the work of moving the camera is less arduous than the work of repainting the art.

(2) The entire picture area should be painted in. Large areas of unpainted, white surface create an amateurish, unartistic look. If necessary, the complexion of the face itself can be left unpainted as long as the features are interesting, and the background is painted in. Often, the background is painted a solid color.

(3) Any feature which is to move should not be painted in unless it is to be covered by a larger cutout. If a child paints in the eyes, they are not movable. However, if the child later decides to have the eyes move, he can cut out two oval pieces of paper to fit and paste one over each eye. Then he can paint two small dark eyeballs on a separate paper and cut them out. These are laid on top of the eyes and then moved under the camera.

A small mouth painted in on the face presents no problem, because larger mouths can be laid on top and animated. At least three different-size mouths are made. One is closed, the other partly open, the third is wide open. These are alternated in sequence when placed on the face and filmed. As a guide, your students should look at each other and see exactly what happens to a mouth when it is open. They should note that there is a dark area between the lips, and that sometimes you can see the teeth or the tongue.

Filming the Art Work

Place the art work on a low table. Set the camera up on the tripod, which should have adjustable legs and a center pole to move the camera height up and down and an adjustable head to tilt the camera vertically. Point the camera down at the art work with the lens from 6 to 18 inches away. (If you are using an 8mm camera, you may not be able to shoot the art work this close to the lens. However, once you have adjusted the distance of lens to art, the basic techniques of filming remain the same.)

If you are using a room with a window that gives good light, you can film using daylight. Otherwise, you must work, as we usually do, in a dark room with photoflood lamps supported by light stands and enhanced by reflectors. You cannot use a combination of outside light and artificial light when filming color because each light source has a different color quality, expressed in degrees Kelvin, the temperature ascribed to it.

When using artificial light, be sure the lamps are the right ones for the type of film in the camera and that the film itself is balanced for tungsten not daylight. These instructions are on the box of film when you buy it. For Ektachrome EF or Ektachrome Commercial, we use two 250-watt photofloods of 3200°K.

Proper positioning of the lights, camera, and art work is essential. The lamps should illuminate the art work evenly. The camera should be directly over the art.

To start, let the first person in the class who has completed painting a face that he likes take it over to the camera and film it. Tell the student that, because the lens is so close to the subject, the camera will probably take in about ¾ of an inch more on all sides than he can see through the viewfinder. He should allow for this margin. It is therefore especially important to get the art work centered under the lens. If the work is not

Typical setup for filming cutout animation has camera on a tripod and pointing down at the art work placed on a low table. Art is illuminated by photofloods in reflectors held by light stands. Jean Falcone is ready to film her art. ▶

SMITH-VICTOR

centered properly, the camera may take in more of the margin than was allowed for and part of the table would be filmed, resulting in what are called "edges." As an aid, the table that holds the art work should have a black top to insure against this. A black edge is not so noticeable when the film is shown in a dark room. A light-colored edge would be noticed.

Next the picture must be focused. For the reflex camera, have the student look through the viewfinder and twist the iris diaphragm control ring on the lens. The student will note that when he twists the diaphragm control ring in one direction, the picture gets light. This is because the diaphragm is performing the same function as the iris of the eye, opening and closing to provide different openings (called apertures) in the lens, and allowing the amount of light entering the camera to be varied. The apertures are termed *f*-stops.

If the student looks at the numbers on the side of the diaphragm control ring, he will then see that a diaphragm setting of *f*/2.8 will give a light picture and a setting of *f*/22 will make it darker. Tell the student to set the diaphragm control ring at the widest aperture to get as much light as possible. The next step is to twist the distance setting ring of the lens so that the picture in the viewfinder looks as sharply focused as possible.

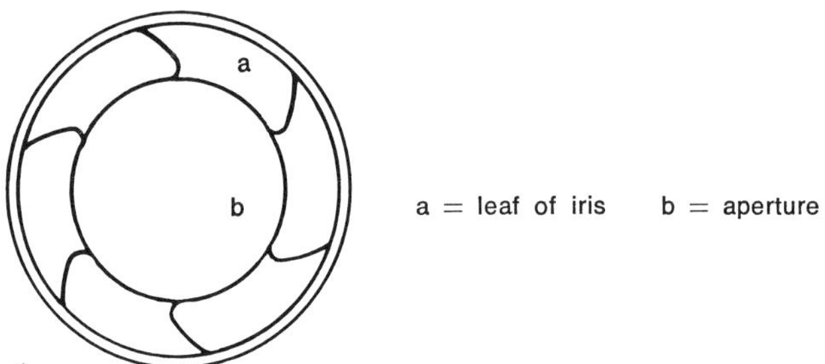

▲ *The leaves of the iris diaphragm in the lens move closer to each other or farther apart, depending on which way you move the control ring. This allows you to control the size of the aperture, and thus the amount of light entering the lens.*

Then the lens opening is stopped down to an aperture that will give the correct exposure.

Cameras with a fixed focus lens or with a separate viewing system require different handling for animation. Methods for their use are given in the last chapter. However, the basic film-making information is the same for all cameras.

Correct Exposure

Exposure depends on two things: the kind of film you are using and the amount of light on the subject. The light meter will measure the latter and show the proper aperture setting for each shooting speed (frames per second).

First, what type of film is in the camera? All films have a different light sensitivity (ASA rating). Ektachrome Commercial is 25 ASA. Ektachrome EF is 125 ASA. The higher the ASA rating of the film, the more sensitive it is to light. You need less light when using Ektachrome EF than when you use Ektachrome Commercial. To get an accurate light reading, you set the ASA window on the light meter to conform to the ASA rating of the film in the camera.

The meter is pointed down at the illuminated art work and a reading is taken. The workshop's animated scenes are shot with the camera set at 16 frames per second—the normal, silent shutter speed for older 16mm cameras. The new standard is 18 frames per second. We use a simple light meter with movie markings on it. (The instruction book that comes with your camera will tell you how to convert frames per second to fractions of a second if you are using a meter calibrated for still cameras. For instance, 16 frames per second usually equals 1/30 of a second in shutter speed.)

The meter has two movable pointers, one of which moves automatically in reaction to the light. Aim the meter at the art work and line up the two pointers. Then, whatever *f*-stop reading is directly across from 16 fps (frames per second) is the correct setting for the diaphragm control ring of the camera.

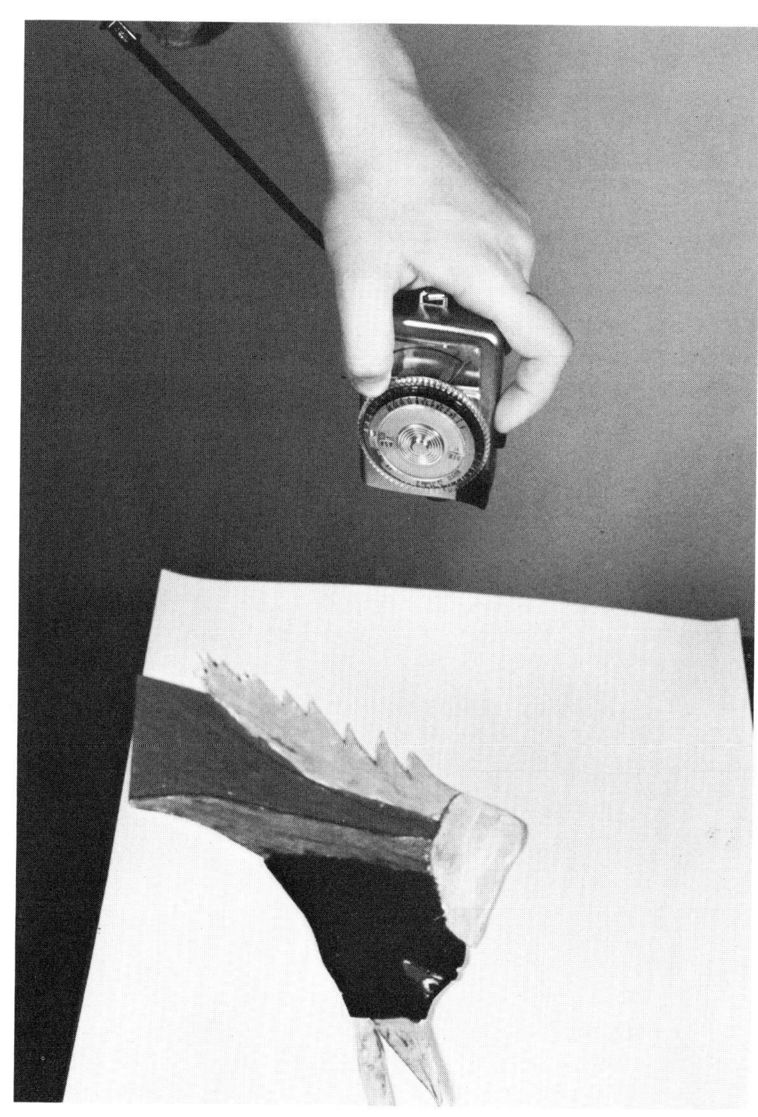

◀ *A light meter is aimed at the art to measure the illumination and tell you how to set the camera for the proper exposure.*

Because animation is filmed with the single-frame release, the camera is functioning as a still camera would and the shutter speed is for the purpose of exposure only, not for capturing motion at the correct speed. Therefore, it is not necessary to film animation at a shutter speed of 16 fps. You can film it at 12 fps, 18 fps, or 24 fps, as long as the diaphragm is open to the correct, corresponding stop, so that the art work is properly exposed.

As far as screen time is concerned, all of the filming done will later be projected with sound at the rate of 24 fps. In order to get one second's worth of movie, you have to take 24 frames. (Most Super 8mm cameras are limited to 18 fps and older 8mm cameras are limited to either 16 fps or 18 fps, which results in a lower quality of sound. In those cases, you shoot 16 or 18 frames for one second of film. The latest 8mm cameras can be shot and projected at 24 fps for sound.)

One more cautionary note about light meters. It is sometimes necessary to take the light reading from a gray card laid down on top of the art work instead of from the art work itself. The reason for this is that sometimes the art has a considerable amount of contrast between light and dark areas. A meter pointed mainly at one area or the other would give you an incorrect reading. A gray card gives you an overall, medium reading.

You cannot judge the exposure by the way the picture looks in the viewfinder after the diaphragm is stopped down. In many reflex viewers the picture appears dark, instead of remaining bright, because less light is being deflected to the viewfinder. Remember you are viewing the art through a series of mirrors set in the camera somewhat like a periscope. If the reflecting mirror is behind the diaphragm instead of in front of it, the small aperture cuts off the light. You are also viewing through ground glass, which makes the image grainy.

The camera and the cutouts are set up for Billy Fuchs, 11, to animate a close-up scene in his film The Idol. *Note the separate hands, mouths and eyelids on the table. Mouths and eyes will open and close; hands will move upward.* ▶

◀ *Peter Bull's cutout figure of "Smirk," based on his earlier portrait, is animated against a painted background that sets the scene for the character's actions.*

Animation

The Face

The student now knows that he must take 24 frames in order to get one second's worth of movie. After he has focused the camera on his art work, he is shown how to press the camera's single-frame release. To begin, he should press the release 24 times without doing any animation so that the filmed face will be seen long enough to register with the audience. Then the animation starts.

If the movable feature is to be the mouth, the first 24 frames are taken with a cutout of the mouth in a closed position. Then the small cutout of the mouth is removed, and is replaced by a medium-sized cutout of a partially open mouth. Two frames are taken. Then the partially open mouth is removed and a large cutout of an open mouth is placed on that spot. Two more frames are taken. The open mouth is removed and the partially open mouth is filmed again for two frames, after which it is replaced by the closed mouth.

This action is repeated back and forth until a total of about 120 frames has been taken. The number of frames taken of each mouth at any one time can vary from 2 frames to 8. The length of the scene will be five seconds, which uses about 3 feet of 16mm film, or 1½ feet of 8mm film. (To convert running time of 8mm, Super 8mm and 16mm, see Table A*.) Five seconds is long enough for a simple animation scene. The character will appear to open and close its mouth. It is not necessary to determine what words are to be spoken. The words will seem to fit later, when you make your sound track.

*page 37

After the student has finished animating and filming the face he painted, he can return to his seat to begin work on his next scene, which will be a full-length figure of the same character in action against a background. Meanwhile, another student will have finished a painting of a face and be ready to film it. With the class properly organized, an even flow of students to and from the camera is maintained, and nobody is left sitting around waiting. The students at their seats will be constantly working on their next scenes or, as work progresses, will be editing rolls of film already processed. Organization in a film class is very important if there are only one or two cameras.

The Figure and Background

The student who has filmed his close-up scene of the face he painted and animated now makes a cutout figure about 7 inches high, including the face—which is a smaller version of the one used for the close-up. This time nothing on the face will move, but the arms and legs of the character will move. The head and body are made in one piece. The arms and legs are separate and are hinged to the underside of the body with tape and thread. The limbs are shaped so they are slightly bent at the elbows and knees, to avoid a stiff look when moving.

Sometimes, only the arms or the legs will be made to move. Then the other limbs can be incorporated in the figure. This is the case with "Smirk," the character from *Cinder City,* who was shown in full-face close-ups on page 14. The figure is a profile cutout which includes one arm extending from the outline of the coat and painted to show the character has his hand in his pocket. Both legs are movable and are attached to the back of the cutout as shown in the black-and-white photograph. Two

◀ *In this series of pictures from Billy Fuchs'* The Idol, *three faces are animated as follows: (1) The filming begins with 24 frames of the faces depicted with the eyes open and the mouths closed. (2) Next the cutout mouths are changed on two characters and hands are added to all three. This setup and the following ones are each filmed for from two to eight frames. (3) The cutout eyelids are placed so they half-cover the eyes. (4) The lids are moved until they completely cover the eyes. (5) Then the eyelids are removed and the mouths are changed again. The hands have been moved upward throughout (6).*

▲
The profile figure of "Smirk" has three parts. Two legs are hinged to the back of the main cutout with tape and thread so the character can be animated to walk. Two other cutouts of the figure show the back and front views of "Smirk."

TABLE A

FILM SIZE	8mm		16mm			Super 8mm	
Projected at	18 fps	24 fps	18 fps	24 fps	16 fps	18 fps	24 fps
Frames per ft.	80	80	40	40	40	72	72
Feet per min.	13.5	18	27	36	24	15	20
Feet per sec.	.225	.3	.45	.6	.4	.25	.33⅓
Inches per sec.	2.7	3.6	5.4	7.2	4.8	3.0	4.0

other cutouts of the character show him from the back and from the front, with both arms incorporated in the figure.

After the character is hinged together, an environment is made for him. Use 11-by-14-inch paper for backgrounds in most cases. Larger backgrounds and characters can be made if the student feels constricted by the 11-by-14-inch format. The trouble with larger backgrounds is that the camera must be farther back from the art. The preferred maximum distance from lens to art is 2½ feet, though you may move as far away as 4 feet. This means that the art may have to be taped to the floor, or the camera may have to be moved up higher. In that case, the animator would have to sit on the floor to move the parts, or the cameraman might have to stand on a chair or ladder.

When the background is made, the student has to consider what the character could do in this background, or what could happen to him. Then this scene is filmed. In the color illustration, "Smirk" is walking by a lamp post.

One of the most frequent actions used will probably be walking. First the scene is filmed by itself for a few frames; then the character walks in, moving forward about ¼ of an inch every two frames. His feet are together for the first two frames; then the right foot is put slightly ahead for the next filming of two frames. The right foot is put even farther ahead for the next two frames. Then the weight of the body seems to rest on the right foot in the succeeding two frames. In the subsequent frames, filmed two at a time, the right foot remains stationary while the left foot closes in. Then the two feet are together again, and the left foot begins to pass the right one. The best way to plan actions of a character is to put yourself in his place, and make him move the way you would.

Organization

Most of the time, workshop students make films separately or in small groups. However, if time and resources are limited, it is best to make the film a group project. In that case, the students would first discuss a possible story and then divide job assignments. These jobs would be: creating characters, backgrounds, and titles; animating the characters; filming; editing; and adding sound.

Every student should work on some portion of the art. Each student should also be responsible for making a character. From these, the main characters are chosen, and the others can be placed in crowd scenes. Crowd scenes are spectacular and effective. The characters are then animated, on a larger background than usual, by three or four students assigned to move them. For titling the credits, each person in the class spells his name out with cutout letters glued onto a large, paper background.

Problems in Filming

(1) As previously mentioned, if the art work is not properly centered, the film may include a picture of the table as well as of the art. These exposed edges may happen on all four sides, one side, or at the top corners. The top corners get edges if the camera is not pointing directly down at the art work, but is at a slight angle. Edges can also happen if someone accidentally kicks the tripod legs during filming.

(2) The younger students usually work in pairs. One pupil operates the camera, while the other youngster animates his own characters. The camera operator must wait until the animator's hands are out of the way before he takes the picture. If hands are accidentally filmed, the frames in which they appear can be edited out, unless they involve too many frames to maintain the sequence.

(3) When the film is processed, you may find the scene too light, with the colors washed out, or too dark, with the correct coloration obscured. This means the proper exposure was not made. Perhaps the light meter was not pointed directly at the art work; the meter may have been angled toward the background or toward either an especially dark or light portion of

the work. You can avoid these problems by using a gray card for taking the meter reading.

(4) If flickering shadows appear, it means that someone moved his arm in between the light and the art work during filming.

(5) Unless you are trying to obtain a special effect, the lighting should remain constant throughout the scene. There are several causes for an unintentional light change in the middle of a scene. Someone may have bumped the light stands, or turned on an overhead light. Also, the camera operator may have filmed part of the scene by live action instead of single-framing. This would cause a darkening of the picture because the camera always exposes a single frame for a fraction of a second longer than it does a frame shot in live action. The instruction book for your camera will have information on this exposure difference.

(6) A fuzzy (unclear) picture is a rare problem if you have a reflex camera that is easy to focus properly. However, the lens of the camera should be kept clean.

(7) A blurred image is due to camera movement. Either the camera was not securely fastened to the tripod, or the tripod was not firmly braced against the table. In single-framing, if the entire picture is blurred, the camera has moved; if only part of the picture is unclear, the camera has not been focused properly. This distinction is difficult to make when filming two-dimensional art but will be evident in later three-dimensional animation.

Look Before You Leap, *by Michael DiGregorio, 14, has a very simple background for this scene. The character, who has just lost all his money at a racetrack, empties his pockets and groans.* ▲

For this scene from Spectator *by Steffen Pierce, 15, the arena is bright pink, with the crowd just roughly sketched in so that the main attention can be focused on the boxers. Cellophane strips pasted on the background represent glistening overhead lights.* ▶

Projection

It is important to get your first roll of film processed and back to class as soon as possible. Rolls of 16mm film are bought in 100-foot lengths. (You get 50 feet in one roll of 8mm film or in one cassette of Super 8mm film.) It takes a long time to shoot 100 feet of animation if most of your scenes are from 3 to 6 feet long. It takes no less time to shoot 50 feet of 8mm or Super 8mm. Remember that 8mm film uses one-half the footage of 16mm film; Super 8mm uses five-ninths the footage of 16mm film. (See Table A, page 37.) Therefore, as soon as each person in the class has filmed a scene, the film should be processed. If the whole roll is not finished, you can shoot it off in a live-action documentary, filming the class preparing art work.

If enthusiasm has lagged at all in the first few classes, it will be instantly revived when the students see their first scenes. The students will learn from the viewing most of what they need to know about improving their animation techniques with cutouts. Some of the scenes will seem shorter than the students had expected them to be. If problems have occurred, the students will see how to correct them. You should orientate your class to the idea that mistakes will be made, since the project is a learning process. Mistakes are made even in professional studios. There could even be some machinery breakdown at the lab, which might result in damaged film.

Projecting their film so they can see the results of their labors inspires the students. It also enables them to spot their errors. Like Jean Falcone, all pupils learn to operate the projector. ▶

All the art work should be carefully saved until the film is completely finished. In case of technical mistakes, or if a student does not like the way his scene turned out, the art can be refilmed. However, do not have the student do any reshooting until the whole film is finished, because the story line may be changed later.

If you have a work print made of the film, you can use this to teach operation of the projector. If the film gets torn, it can easily be replaced by having another copy made from the original. Each time a new roll of film comes back from the lab, have a different student load it up on the projector to learn how. The manual-threading rather than the self-threading type of projector is preferable, because it is less apt to tear student-made splices.

During projection, there will be screams of delight, such as, "It turned out just the way I wanted it to!" There will also be groans for technical mistakes. However, the teacher should make sure that no student remains dejected because of filming errors in his scene. Remind the student that the scene can be refilmed later, and that he learns from his errors.

In refilming a scene, the student should not merely duplicate the animation he did in his first attempt. He should take advantage of the opportunity to do the scene in a new and better way, artistically as well as technically. It is boring to merely redo a scene. Often a scene that has to be redone for technical reasons ends up better than it would have if it had been correct the first time. Also consider the fact that it is much easier to refilm an animation scene than a live-action one. You simply have to get together the art work instead of a collection of actors, scenery, the right weather, etc.

A manual-threading projector allows the film to be fed by hand from the right-hand reel through the film gate (arrow) and onto the left-hand take-up spool, passing around various sprocketed and unsprocketed rollers. An automatic-threading machine does not allow the operator such easy access to the film in case something causes it to get caught in the projector. ▶

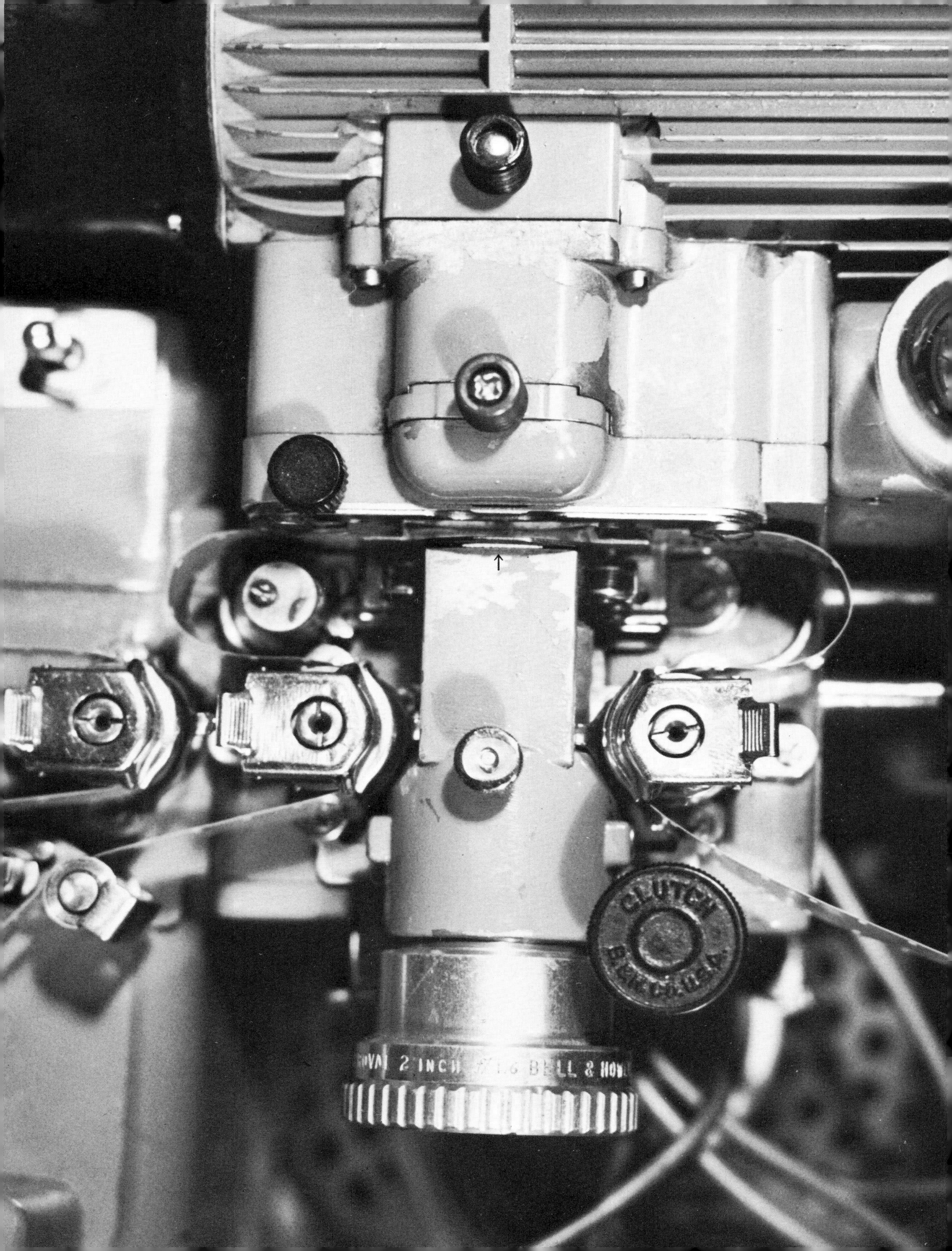
CLUTCH
2 INCH
BELL &

Editing and Splicing

Editing

Each time a roll of film returns from the lab, some students are assigned to edit it, eliminating bad footage, and cutting and arranging the scenes in their proper sequence. If the members of the class are working on separate films, each student must eventually cut his own footage out of the roll and splice it onto his previous film work. For this procedure, the class needs an editing set with a splicer.

An editing set consists of a viewer through which the film is passed by cranking it from the reel on the left to the take-up reel on the right. Both reels are held by cranking devices called rewinds. The splicer is a separate tool for accurately cutting and joining one piece of film to another. An editing set has the splicer joined to it, but you can get a separate editor and add a more expensive splicer.

The student loads the roll of film onto the set's left-hand rewind, through the viewer and onto the take-up reel on the right side of the editor. He winds the film through, watching the scenes in the viewer. When he comes to the beginning of his own scene, he pulls the film out of the viewer and cuts with a scissors through the middle of his first frame. He then attaches a piece of masking tape to this part (the head) of his film, which he tapes to the edge of the worktable. He unrolls the next few feet of film from its reel and views it by available light until he comes to the end of his scene. Next, he cuts through the last frame of his scene and lets this portion (the tail) drop into a clean paper bag on the floor. He then splices together the ends of the film left on the two reels and rewinds the spliced film back onto the left reel, which he removes. The removed film reel will be used later by each of the other students in exactly the same way.

◀ *Author-instructor Yvonne Andersen shows Kathy Ahern, 16, where strip of film will be cut. In front of Kathy is a splicing machine to join two cut ends of film.*

Once the student has removed his own section of film, he edits it further, inserting it into his previous footage. If this is his first footage, he attaches about 6 feet of black leader film to the editor's right-hand take-up reel. Then he splices the head of his scene to the tail of this leader, and winds the film forward. When he reaches the tail of the footage, he splices 4 feet of black leader film onto that. The tail of this leader is taped to the editor's left take-up reel and the whole film is re-wound into start position. The film is now ready to be projected.

The purpose of the black leader is for threading the film into the projector. The paper bag is to keep the film free from dust. Even a very tiny piece of dust can damage a film when it is caught in the film gate of the projector. Each week, when new scenes return from the lab, each student adds in the new footage for his own film, resplicing the leaders when necessary. Before a student does any editing at all, he learns how to make a splice.

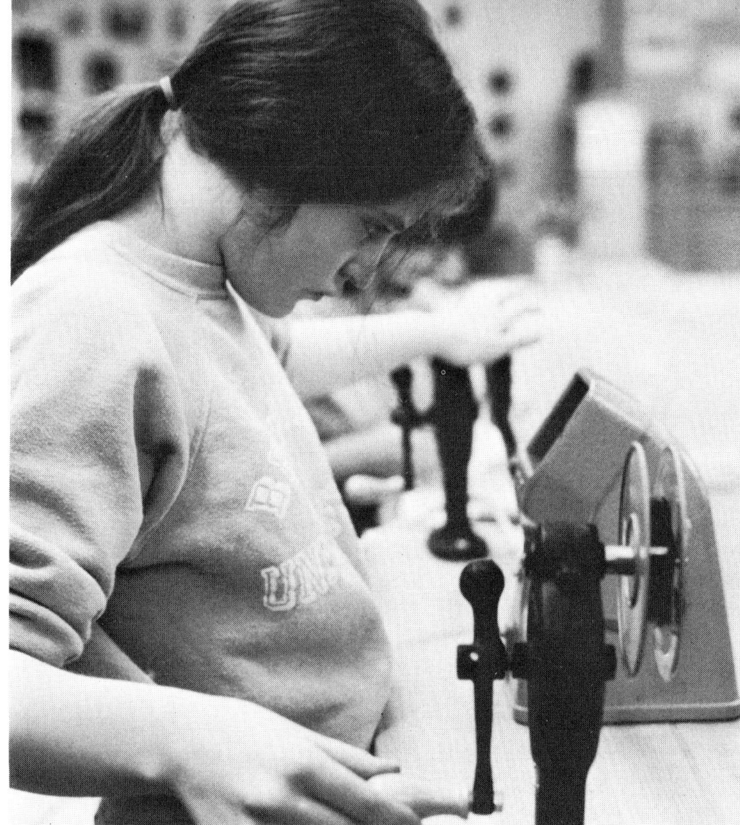

▲
Amy Kravitz, 13, examines film in the viewer of the editing set. The rewind on the right holds the take-up spool; the one on the left holds the reel of film.

Splicing

The teacher demonstrates how to splice, using scraps of film for the purpose. The student must make at least two perfect splices by himself on scrap film before he works on the animated film.

There are two basic ways to make a splice: dry splicing with tape, and wet splicing with cement. Splicing tapes are available in either perforated or unperforated form. Both tapes make a butt splice in which the two ends of the film are cut and joined along the frame line. A guillotine splicer uses unperforated tape, which is pressed over the splice area and is perforated by the top handle of the splicer. Other splicers use perforated tape. Small, projecting pins hold the two pieces of film in alignment while you press the tape over the adjoining frames. The film should be turned over and taped on the other side, too.

Cement splicers are somewhat more complicated. Guide pins and pressure plates hold the two pieces of film in place in such a way as to make an overlapping joint instead of a butt splice. This means that a part of the frame to be overlapped must have the emulsion (the dull, color-coated side) scraped away, so it will make a firm bond with the base side (shiny side) of the overlapping portion from the other piece of film.

The bond is made with a special cement, and the emulsion is scraped away either with a built-in device on the splicer or with a razor blade. In the latter case, the emulsion is first moistened. Each cement splicer has its own instructions, but the basic technique is the same in all splicers of this type. In addition, some more expensive cement splicers have a heating element to help weld the two pieces of film. This is called hot splicing.

By assembling your own editing setup from separate components instead of using an editor that includes the splicer, you gain flexibility but you also increase the cost. For instance, the guillotine splicer pictured here costs about $185. It makes butt splices (the film ends do not overlap) and uses unperforated tape at a cost of about $1.50 per roll. The advantage of this splicer is that it is very easy to use. The teacher has only to demonstrate it once, and the student can almost always make a foolproof splice immediately. The tape is applied to both sides of the film.

The tape splice can be taken apart by just peeling off the tape. New scenes can be inserted without losing any frames, as would happen if your splices were overlapped and cemented. This splicer was designed especially for use in splicing 16mm magnetic, sprocket-holed sound tape, but the workshop also uses it for splicing work prints and repairing torn sprocket holes in damaged film. This splicer is our real workhorse, but it should not be used for splicing original film because the thickness of the tape shows up at both ends of the splice as a difference in focus when the film is projected. Use a cement splicer for original film.

The Craig Master Six Splicer costs $13.00 and can make good splices using either tape or cement on 8mm, Super 8mm or 16mm. The advantages of this splicer are its low cost and its flexibility.

The Maier-Hancock Portable Hot Splicer, Model 816, for 16mm and 8mm costs about $250. It is a very fine professional splicer to be used with cement. It gives a very good, almost invisible splice. We use it for splicing original film. However, such professional equipment is not essential; an ordinary cement splicer will do the job if used with care.

Possible Problems

When a newly spliced film jams or loses its loop in the projector, the difficulty is usually caused by a bad splice. In cement splicing, if the emulsion side of the film has not been thoroughly scraped off, and if either the base or emulsion side is not clean

▲ *This versatile Craig Master splicer can make tape splices or the more difficult cement splices. The cement splice results in a loss of one frame, because each end of the two film strips to be joined must be cut inside the frame line and properly aligned so that one end overlaps the other film strip just the right amount.*

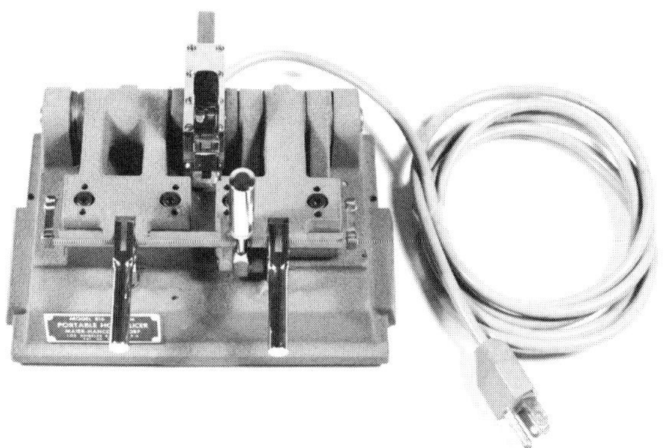

▲ *The hot splicer uses heat to help weld the cement splice firmly.*

◀ *The guillotine splicer requires only a roll of unperforated splicing tape to make butt joints between two pieces of film, each cut on the frame line. When pressed down, as it is here, the handle perforates the tape to form a sprocket hole.*

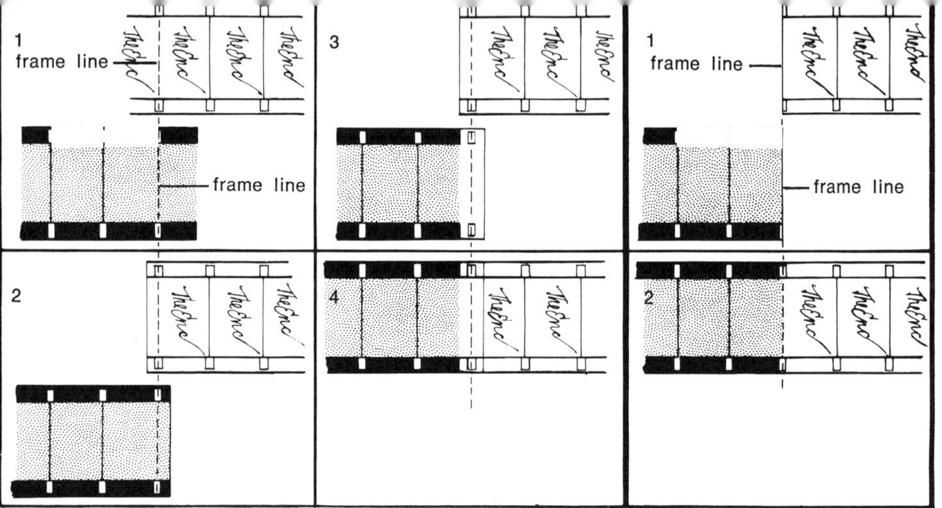

For cement splicing: (1) Place film in splicer aligned as shown. (2) Cut both sides of film in splicer with precision cut. (3) Scrape film in left side of splicer, and apply cement to scraped portion. (4) Bring down film in right side of splicer and press on top of film at left side. Note that the picture on the left is missing part of its image and has a little of the right picture in it. This will not matter if splice is made and projected properly.
For tape splicing: (1) Film can be cut on frame line to avoid loss of frames. (2) Ends are butted together and tape is over-lapped on both sides. Use perforated tape or a guillotine splicer. Tape may be peeled off to change positions of scenes without losing frames.

and dry before the cement is applied, the splice will not hold. In either cement or tape splicing, it may be that the ends of the film were not properly aligned or were not cut precisely. In tape splicing, it is possible that only one side of the film was taped.

If a film which has been run through the projector is found to be incorrectly spliced together, the student should take it back over to the editing setup and correct it immediately. Each week, as more scenes are returned, the student adds the new scenes into his own reel of previous footage, placing the scenes in approximate order. If he has used a tape splicer, the old tape splices can be peeled off to insert a new scene, and no frames are lost. A cement splicer causes a loss of one frame per splice and two frames each time footage is inserted (two splices).

An obvious mishap is when the picture on the screen appears upside down or backwards. This can be caused by a student's not having rewound the film back into starting position after he has edited it. Since the film is fed from left to right on most editors, the starting position is usually the left-hand reel. Before splicing a piece of film, the student should hold it up to the editor's viewer light. The top or head of a person in a scene should be on your right; the feet on your left. If the film has edge numbers, the numbers will be on the top edge of the film, along with the perforations.

Edge numbers are very good to have if you are working with an original and a work print. They are numbers on one side of the original film which are printed through onto the work print. The lab will have to be informed that you want to have the edge numbers. During editing and sound synchronization, the work print is used and the original film is preserved until the end. Then the original film is spliced to conform exactly, frame for frame, with the work print. The edge numbers on both films are very useful when you do this work. The original is then taken back to the lab, and all future prints are made from it.

Having a work print is a good idea if you expect to be showing your film often. Film scratches easily during the many projections necessary in editing it and in making the sound track. All this heavy work is done on the work print. All release prints for public showing are made from the unscratched original film. The disadvantage of the work print is the cost. It doubles the cost of the film work.

If you have the resources, you should plan to have either a work print or timed copy. A work print is a copy which is not timed very carefully for the exposure of each scene. Some of the scenes may look lighter than they will on the original. The workshop often decides to have a timed copy to edit with. Here, any variation in exposure from scene to scene is corrected in the print. This costs a little more, but shows you exactly how the color will be in the final print.

The storyboard is a rough sketch of the scenes and their sequence in the movie. This is Deirdre Cowden's storyboard for her film Smoke! Smoke!, *made when she was 13. Scenes of the final movie appear in color on page 51.*

Story

A classic example of the development of a film from the creation of a face, a figure, and a background to the telling of a story is the evolution of *Smoke! Smoke!* by Deirdre Cowden, age 13. The first scene painted was the face. It showed a man with dark bushy hair, a bulbous nose, a moustache, and heavy eyebrows. He had a pipe in his mouth and he looked somewhat like a college professor. The scene was filmed. Four elements moved: the blue eyeballs went from side to side, the cutout moustache rose up and down, as did the pipe, and puffs of gray smoke drifted out of the pipe.

Then Deirdre painted a smaller copy of the man's face and added his body. He was dressed in an orange shirt, green vest, and purple-checkered pants. He looked like a cowboy. This time no facial features moved, but his arms and legs did.

Next, Deirdre painted a background for him. It was a yellow kitchen with a red stove on which a pot of spaghetti was cooking. The man was a cook in an Italian restaurant. Deirdre then decided to show the restaurant from the outside. She spent a long time creating a beautiful street scene with Cray-Pas crayons and paint. It showed a cobblestone road, a sidewalk, people, and traffic. The viewpoint was from high above eye level, looking partly down on the street, and the restaurant sign was in the corner. It read, "Italiano Restuaranto" (misspelled, but picturesque). The movement in this scene begins with a red car; it drives by with its rotatable wheels turning. A thin man in a green suit crosses the street and enters the restaurant.

The next scene is the restaurant interior with tables and chairs. The walls are wood finish. The tablecloths are blue. A man in a yellow shirt sits in the center of the room gobbling spaghetti. The food is actually a long strand of string painted to look like tomato-covered spaghetti. The man's arm and his hand, in which he holds a fork, move up and down together, shoveling gobs of spaghetti into his mouth. He eats by sucking the string into a punch-hole in his mouth. The animator has only to pull the string, which comes out on the underside of the painted, paper setting.

In the background, behind the spaghetti-eater, we see the man in the green suit who previously entered the restaurant. He just sits and waits. After this "long shot" showing all the action in the room, the camera cuts to a "close-up" of the uncouth yellow-shirted man sucking his spaghetti. On the sound track, there is a noisy sucking sound. The camera then cuts to a close-up shot of the green-clothed man, who has a look of disdain on his face. There is no animation in the close-up.

If the student spends a lot of time making elaborate scenery, as Deirdre does, many different shots and animation can be done with just one scene. This extends the time of the film and takes full advantage of every item of interest in such a scene. To do this, you have only to move the camera in closer.

Now Deirdre has taken the shots which we could call documentary. She has stated a time, place, and characters and has

A color sequence from Deirdre Cowden's film Smoke! Smoke! *shows how the portrait of the main character, the various backgrounds, and the cutout figures are all brought together to tell a story.* ▶

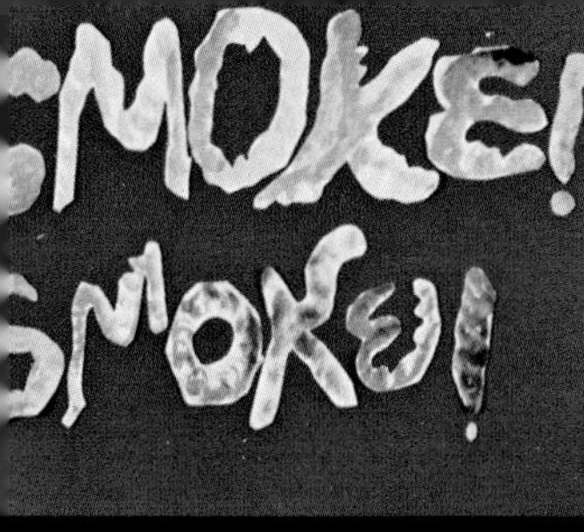
MOKE!
SMOKE!
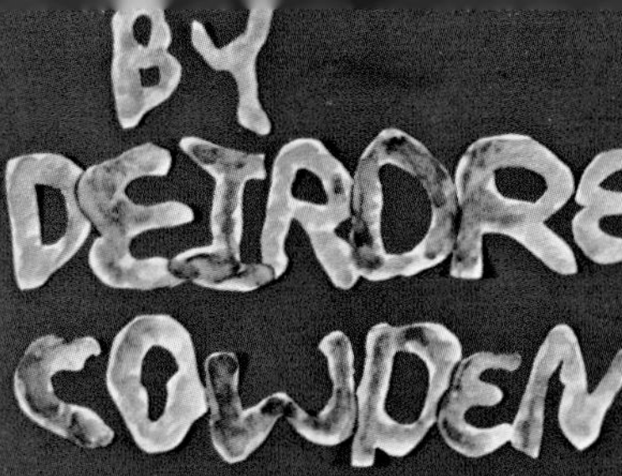
BY
DEIRDRE
COWDEN

ITALIAN
RESTVAR
ANTO

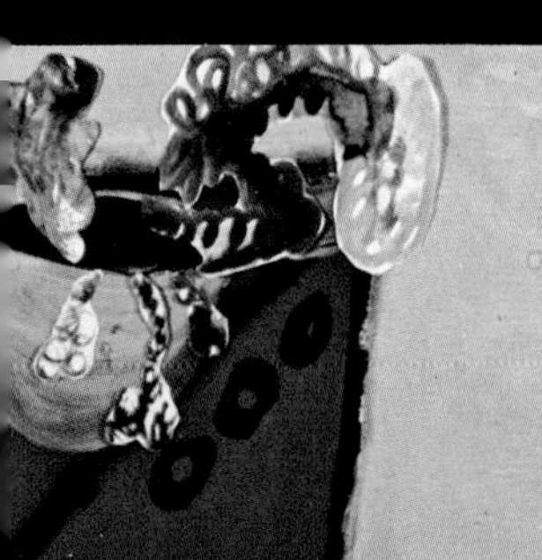

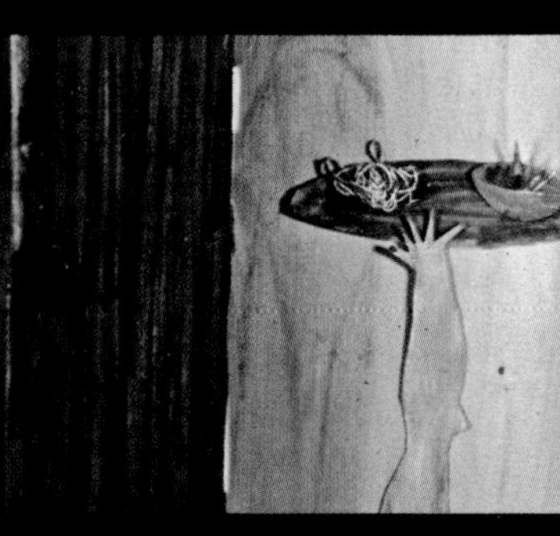
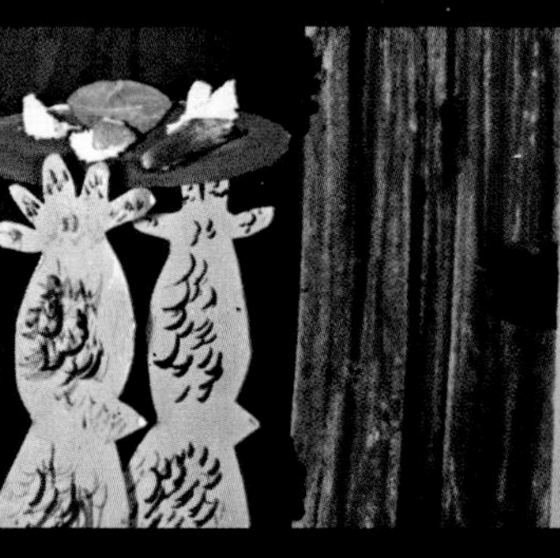

ITALIAN
RESTVAR
ANTO

THE END

examined the surroundings. The next step is to devise some sort of climax or important event which might take place. Deirdre decided to have the pot of spaghetti boil over. She had already filmed the cook smoking his pipe. Deirdre concluded she would have the cook so busy smoking his pipe that he forgets to mind the pot of spaghetti, and it boils over.

She painted a close-up scene of the stove with the pot on it, and painted many cutout pieces of smoke and foul-looking drippings to slide down the side of the pot. This scene was filmed, exaggerating the event to its fullest degree. Then Deirdre re-filmed the original kitchen background, this time with the cook discovering the pot. In this scene, he is facing forward and his eyes are large white circles with pinpoint black eyeballs in the center to show amazement. His hands are moving in the air, and smoke is rapidly filling the room.

When reminded that she had not shown the waitresses in the restaurant, Deirdre felt that it was too much work to make more characters. She decided to show only the most important part of them. She would show only their arms, high in the air, carrying trays of food back and forth through a swinging door.

Deirdre painted a sheet of paper yellow on the right half, to be the kitchen interior, and brown on the left half, for the dining room. She then cut out a piece of paper and painted it on both sides with a wood grain. This would be the door opening and closing between the kitchen and dining room. This door was hinged to the background.

The next step was to make a pair of hairy forearms representing the busboy. The arms, holding a tray of dirty dishes high above his head, are the only parts of him seen as he enters the kitchen. Another set of arms represented each waitress carrying a tray of food through the doorway.

The scene was filmed in three parts. The brown door swings open and a waitress comes out of the kitchen with the dinner. Immediately, the door swings the other way and the busboy goes into the kitchen with a load of dirty dishes. Then the door swings open for another waitress, but smoke is pouring out of the kitchen behind her. The smoke encircles the waitress, and the tray and the dinner fall down, crashing to the floor. On the sound track, we hear the dishes breaking.

Next the dining room is refilmed and we see the diners encircled with smoke. Then the exterior of the restaurant is shown. The green-suited man dashes out and is followed by smoke. The gray smoke fills the whole scene. The background is changed to red, and the words "The End" form from gray smoke.

A beautiful and complex background was painted for Move, Kid *by Kathy Ahern, 16. The people in the crowd walk by, and one man in an orange coat climbs the stairs.* ▶

Special Techniques in Cutout Animation

Snow and Rain

Falling snow can be created by cutting out dozens of little separate white balls and animating them downward on top of the art work. Every two frames, each ball must be moved downward ¼ of an inch. If there is a character moving through the snow, use three animators—one to move the character, and the other two to move the snow. Once the falling snow hits the white ground, remove it from the scene and place it at the top of the art work to begin its descent again. This same technique can be used for rain.

An easier method is to use a double exposure, superimposing the snow or rain onto the scene. First film the scene without the snow or rain. During this filming, close the diaphragm down ½ stop to slightly decrease the light, darkening the scene so the snow will show up. Then place a lens cap over the lens, and rewind the film in the camera back to the starting place for that scene. Paint a long black scroll with white specks resembling particles of snow. Place the painted scroll under the camera, and film it, rolling it forward ¼ of an inch every two frames.

With a scroll, the snow particles do not have to be moved separately. The exposure should be only enough for the white particles to register on the film, leaving the black background so underexposed that no tone at all registers. The scroll should also be filmed with the lens diaphragm closed down ½ stop more than the reading for it. You must check the footage counter of the camera to be sure that you start and end both scenes at identical points. This same technique can be used for rain. However, it can be used only with cameras which can be back-wound.

◀ *To give the illusion of falling rain or snow, each particle is cut out and animated downward. This scene is from* The Park People, *done as a group project.*

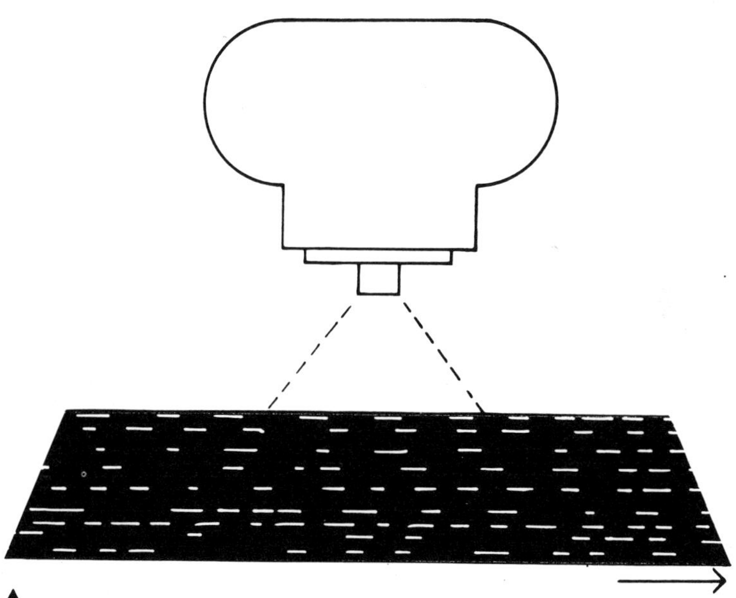

▲ *To simplify the animation of a rainfall or a snowfall, a black scroll with the particles painted on is rolled forward under the camera lens.*

Fire and Smoke, Explosive Displays, Waves

The illusion of fire is produced by a series of cutout flames. The flames must be totally changed every two frames in order to maintain the flickering effects of fire. Different sizes of smoke clouds changed every two frames create a billowing effect. A single smoke puff can also be animated moving upward to get a drifting effect.

Explosions are usually shown by using three different-sized cutouts, which can be a jagged sunburst shape or puffs of smoke. They are filmed in this sequence: the small cutout (two frames), the medium cutout (two frames), the large cutout (two frames), the medium cutout (two frames), the small cutout (two frames).

Lightning and fireworks are done the same way, using appropriately shaped cutouts. Each time a new cutout is filmed, the one before it has to be removed.

The same idea of appropriately shaped cutouts is used for ocean waves. You need at least two strips of paper with waves cut in them. The strips must be longer than the picture area. Every two frames, the alternate strips of waves are pulled ¼ of an inch in opposite directions from each other.

▲
Different-sized cutouts of smoke, or of other appropriate shapes, are filmed in alternation to give special effects for fires, explosions, and even bursts of lightning.

▲
Two strips of waves moved in opposite directions create the action of the ocean. (Scene is from Underwater Creatures, *made by Paul Falcone at age 6.)*

The main character, shown in a close-up on the next page, is a hippy and is harrassed by "square" people in The Enlightenment, *by Mark Winer, and Larry Stern, both 17. Rather than paint an entire city scene, the two boys used photographs cut from magazines for the skyscraper environment.* ▶

Cutouts from Magazines

Scenes cut from magazine photographs are fun to film and animate. They are especially useful if the students feel inadequate about their drawing and painting abilities. The combination of painted characters and magazine sets are particularly charming.

In a scene from *The Enlightenment,* by Mark Winer, 17, and Larry Stern, 17, several magazine cutouts are used to create a city. The film is about a hippy who feels that he is constantly pressured to conform to "square" standards. He is pursued down alleyways and in all parts of the city by people screaming at him. "Cut your hair! Pinko! Freak. Why don't you get a job!" they yell. He is finally thrown into jail, where he sobs to himself, "Why are all these people after me? I give up! I give up!"

The picture of the hippy slowly dissolves (fuses) into one of a heavier hippy and then into one of a tough top sergeant. The next scene cuts to a war zone. Two soldiers shoot at each other. The sergeant screams, "Kill!" A bomb explodes. A bloody hand reaches up into the scene, and the voice whispers again, "Kill! Kill . . ."

This is an extremely powerful first film by two teen-age young men facing the draft. They spent a lot of time discussing different endings to the film, and finally chose this one.

The film *Just a Fishment of My Imagination* evolved primarily from magazine cutouts of eyes and mouths. Carol Sones, 17, cut the photographs of eyes and mouths from magazines and merely looked at them for several lessons. Then she started changing them. The natural shape of the eyes suggested a fish shape. She made a fish whose whole body was primarily an eye cutout. Another fish's face was all mouth. In the film this fish laughs a lot. Then Carol incorporated both eyes and mouths into different fish bodies.

Carol's entire film, except for the first scene, was filmed through a glass dish of water. In the first scene, a lady sits facing the camera; in front of her is a fishbowl. A cutout fish is animated so it appears to swim in the bowl. The lady bends her head down to look at the fish in the bowl. The movement of her head is animated with a series of four different cutouts. Each head position is filmed for four frames. Upon reaching the final frame of the cutout which shows the top of the lady's head, the scene dissolves into one showing a close-up of the lady's face as it might be seen through water by a fish. This close-up scene and all the remaining ones were filmed through water, using the special technique that follows.

Underwater Effect

The art work is on a low table or the floor. The camera, on a tripod, points down at it. In between the camera and the art is a glass dish of water. The dish rests on two sticks of wood. One end of each stick is taped to the tripod. The other end of each stick rests on a box on the other side of the art.

The special setup for filming through water also requires a black shield between the camera and the water, otherwise the camera might film a reflection of itself in the water. This shield

Cutouts of eyes and mouths from magazine photographs provided ▶ *the inspiration for these fish characters by Carol Sones, 17, for her movie* Just a Fishment of My Imagination.

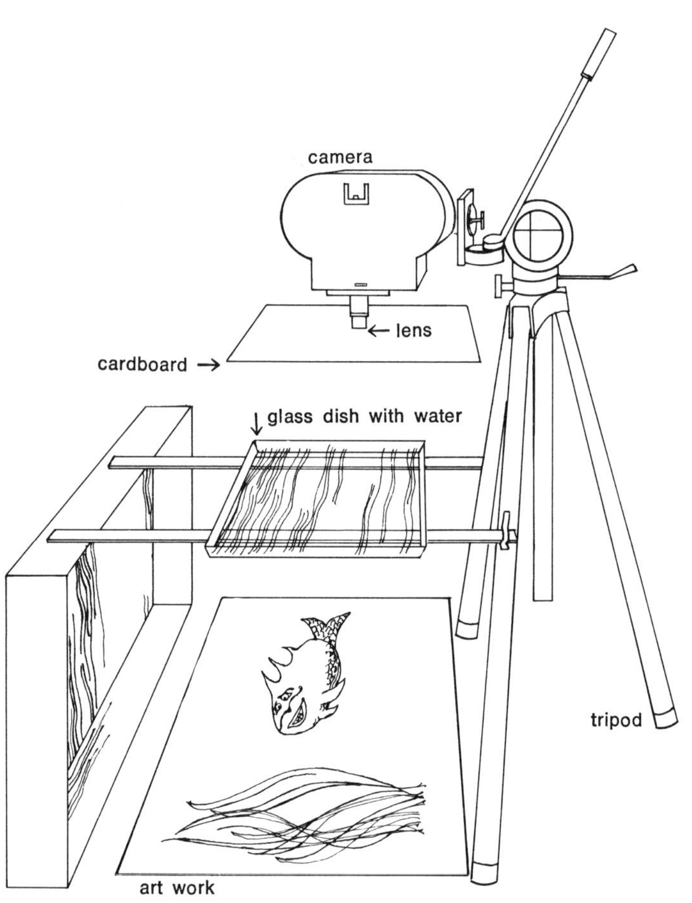

is a piece of cardboard which must be black on the side facing toward the water. The camera lens protrudes through a small round hole cut in the middle of this shield. The cardboard is held onto the camera by the rim of an adapter ring, which is screwed into the lens after the cardboard shield is on. This adapter ring is the same kind used for attaching filters or close-up lens onto the front of the camera.

In filming the scene, the photographer dips his finger into a corner of the glass dish, and wiggles the water a little. While the water is wiggling, he takes two frames. This rippling water causes the underwater effect. The characters animated against the art work in the film are cutouts.

If you cannot find a large glass-bottomed dish, you can take a sheet of picture glass and build up a plasteline wall along each side of the glass rectangle to keep the water in. Make each wall about 3 inches high, and join them together.

Transition from Scene to Scene

A movie is made up of many scenes (episodes). There are four basic ways to make a transition between scenes. The simplest is called a cut. One scene stops abruptly and another begins. This is the method most often used.

A second method is called a fade-out. The scene gradually gets darker until the screen is completely black. You do this by progressively closing down the lens diaphragm ⅓ stop every two frames, until you have closed down the lens opening four entire stops. For the final few frames, cover the lens with the lens cap.

Similarly, a fade-in is created when the screen starts out black and gradually lightens to the correct exposure as the scene

◀ *The setup for shooting an underwater scene includes a large, glass dish of water placed between the camera and the art work. A sheet of colored cardboard must be fastened to the camera with its black side facing the water.*

appears. You start by taking a few frames with the lens cover on, or with your hands covering the lens. Then progressively open the lens diaphragm ⅓ stop every two frames until you get to the correct *f*-stop for exposing the scene.

A dissolve is created when one scene seems to melt or blend into another. To do this, fade-out on the first scene. Then wind the film in the camera back to the start of the fade-out and fade-in the second scene on top of the first scene.

Zoom

Sometimes you can create the feeling of movement by handling the camera instead of by animating the art work. A "zoom in" gives the effect of moving closer to the scene. A "zoom out" gives the opposite effect. This is easily accomplished if you have a zoom lens. If you do not have a zoom lens, you have to create the effect manually by moving the camera position every two frames.

In order to hold the camera stationary while filming and yet be able to move it forward in a steady progression every two frames, it is helpful to mount the camera on the runner of an old, inexpensive titling stand. This is the only part of the titling stand you need. Place the runner and camera on a table next to the wall. Tape the art work onto the wall in front of the camera. The camera can be moved forward or backward on the runner.

Make a few dry runs with the camera zooming in and out from the art work to be sure everything is centered. Then you are ready. As you move in for the zoom, take two frames every ¼ of an inch that the camera moves forward. Move the camera forward until you get the picture you want.

When it has been moved about 2 inches, the camera has to be refocused. The diaphragm control ring is opened completely, the focusing ring is changed, and the diaphragm is closed back down to its correct setting for the light. Then the camera can be moved forward again in ¼-inch steps for another 2 inches before refocusing is required. This is a rather arduous process, and should be done only if it is absolutely necessary to the story or to the flow of the film. The zoom scene illustrated is from *Yellow Submarine,* by Elsa Glassman, 16.

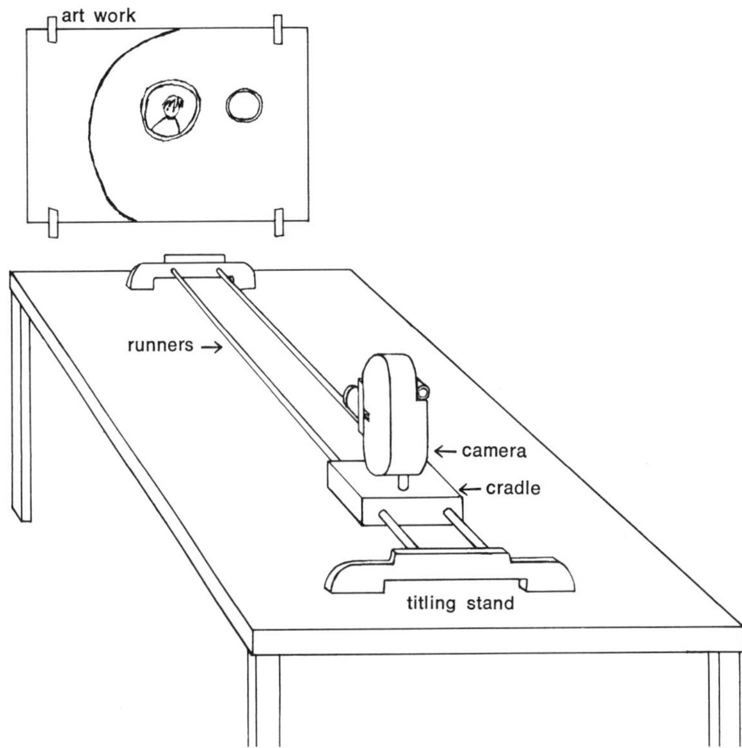

▲
Zooming in on the scene produces the effect of moving the viewer closer to the scene. If the camera does not have a zoom lens, the camera itself must be moved forward in a very controlled way. Fastening the camera to the track of a titling stand is a good method.

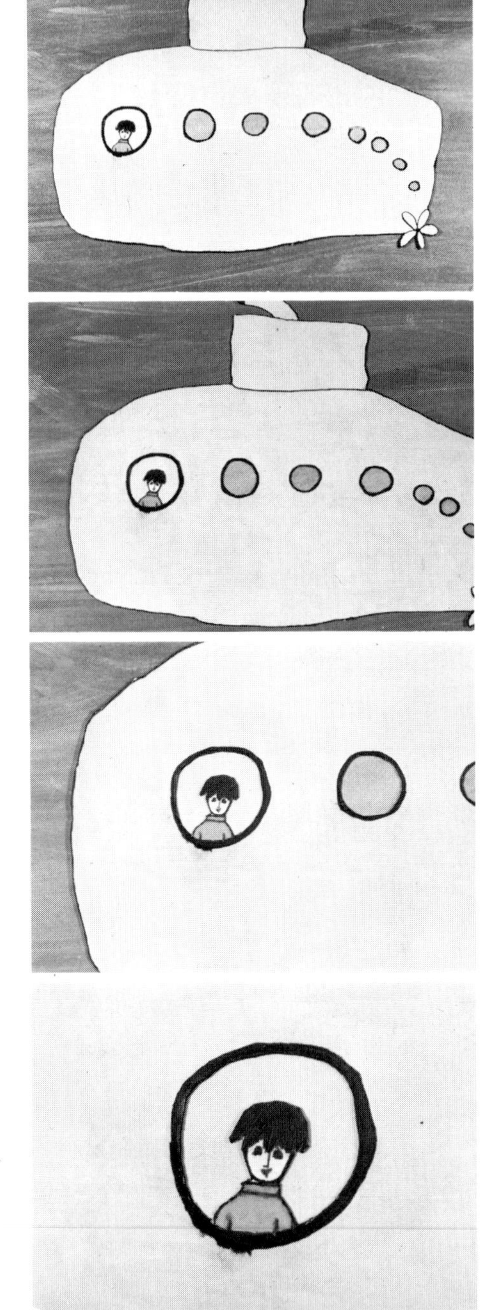

This zoom sequence is from Yellow Submarine, *by Elsa Glassman, 16.* ▶

Pan

A pan in live-action filming refers to the action of swinging a camera slowly across a landscape or a crowd of people in order to show a wide-ranging horizontal or vertical area. In cut-out animation, the camera does not move for the pan. The art work is moved under the camera.

The art is usually a long, horizontal strip which is slowly moved under the camera about ⅛ of an inch every two frames, either to the right or to the left. Two strips of wood tacked so that one adjoins the top of the art work and the other adjoins the bottom will allow it to be moved smoothly. In a case where the camera seems to pan buildings or landscapes, and there is no further action, a pan is a simple thing. It becomes more complex if there are moving characters on this landscape.

In most cases the moving character is a person who is walking. The character appears to walk forward, always remaining in the center of our view while the background slips by behind him. Two people usually animate a scene like this. One moves the background backwards ⅛ of an inch every two frames. The other animates the character to make him walk. This second animator must make constant checks through the camera's viewfinder to keep the character centered. The effect in the finished film is that of a mobile camera following a walking person.

In the film *Move, Kid,* by Kathy Ahern, 16, a boy and a dog walk slowly down the street. The camera follows them. Meanwhile, on top of the traffic noise, we hear a panting sound. It is a runner. He enters the scene swiftly, catching up with the boy, who is in his way. He grunts hoarsely, "Move, Kid," and shoves the boy out of his way and into the street.

This was a difficult scene because four elements were all moving at different speeds: the background, the boy, the dog, and the runner. When the boy is hit, he flips head over heels out of the picture on the bottom right side. The film cuts to the next scene, which shows a truck screeching to a stop just a few inches in front of the boy.

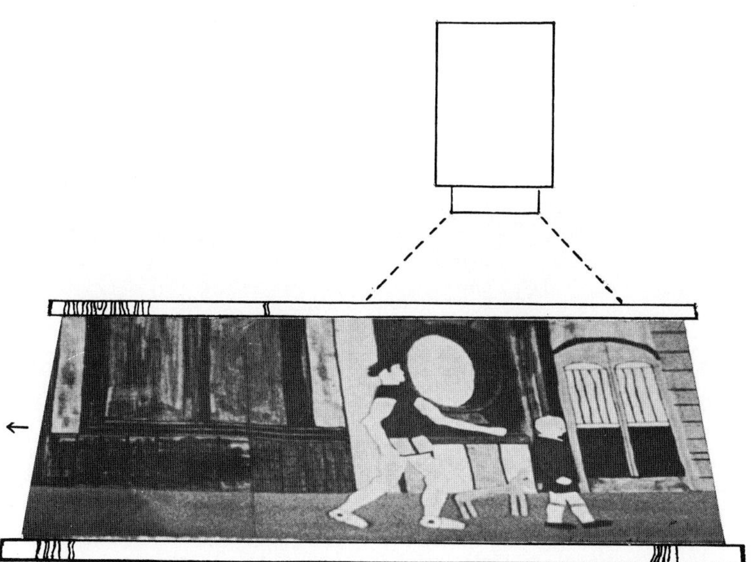

◀ *In an animated pan, the background is moved backward to give the effect that the camera is following the characters. The camera actually remains stationary. The characters may also be animated at the same time. (Scene is from* Move, Kid.*)*

A complicated scene from Kathy Ahern's Move, Kid *uses a background that is longer than usual so that the camera can be centered on the action of the three characters in a pan.* ▶

Movement Toward and Away from the Camera

The truck in *Move, Kid* could have been animated as a speck in the distance, getting larger and larger as it comes toward the camera. This would have required the making of about eight different-sized trucks, but we used an easier method. Kathy made just the one truck and animated it into the scene rather swiftly, starting with the wheels at the top of the frame and moving the truck downward about ½ of an inch every two frames. The boy was animated to fall out into its path just before it almost hits him.

The film cuts to an extreme close-up on the driver's face. His mouth is opening and closing as he yells, "What are you doing in the street! You're not supposed to be in the street! Get back on the sidewalk and don't do that again!" It is a very effective scene with the screech of the tires, the honk of the horn, and the driver's voice.

An example of a more complex way to animate an object toward or away from the camera is shown in another scene from *Move, Kid.* This time the boy and his dog walk up from the bottom of the screen and continue up a hill, getting smaller and smaller as they move farther away. When they reach the top of the hill, they seem to walk over the top and down the other side, disappearing from view.

The boy and the dog were each made in five decreasing sizes. The five dog cutouts were made in two parts. The front part is an inverted "U" shape with a head and ears, and the back part

◀ *The boy in the previous scene is knocked by the runner into the path of an oncoming truck, which halts just in time. The truck's movement toward the boy and the camera was animated by positioning the front wheels at the top of the frame and advancing the entire truck downward 1/2 of an inch every two frames.*

Walking up a hill, the boy and his dog are moving away from the camera. This scene was animated by using five different cutouts with movable parts for each of the characters. ▶

is another inverted "U" shape. In walking, the back "U" shape was moved toward the front one, which was then moved forward, away from the back one. The cutouts of the boy were each one piece from the head to the edge of the pants legs. The legs were all separate so that they could be animated.

To show the movement of stepping forward, the leg taking the step was slid up under its pants leg. Every few steps the larger character was removed and replaced with a smaller one. When the boy was standing on the top of the hill, a slit was made in the background paper along the line of the hilltop. The boy's feet were placed into the slit and he was animated downward until he disappeared from view.

Titling

Titling is an important film feature. It includes giving the name of the film, the name of the artist and some indication at the end to let the audience know that the film is over. Some students are very involved in the main action of the film and think that they do not need a title. Without one, however, you have no way of referring to the film. Also the first thing the audience sees is the title. This sets the tone for the rest of the film.

The title should be short, visually exciting, and related to the film. In *Atomic Robot,* by Paul Falcone, 8, there is a white background. The atomic robot scuttles out into the scene sideways, facing the audience with a heap of cutout letters in his arms. He lays the letters out across the screen one by one, spelling the title, in tune to an electronic beat in the music. Then with one blow, he smashes the letters into a pile, and reassembles them to read: "by Paul Falcone." (See color page 76.)

The simplest type of titling is to paint three sheets of paper a solid color and, when the papers are dry, to paint the title on one sheet, the name of the artist on another, and "The End" on

◀ *Each cutout of the boy was a progressively smaller size, and each allowed the legs to be animated for walking.*

the third. Cutout letters can be well-positioned on the paper, and even animated. With a bit more art work, the title can be made both provocative and an integral part of the film. For example, in a film called *The Amazing Colossal Man,* a space ship in the sky writes the title in white smoke against a blue background. The ship continues its flight to earth through a field of varicolored stars. The stars have the names of the students who made the film written on them.

One of the first complex titling sequences done by workshop students was for *$50,000 Per Fang,* by Steve DeTore, 13, assisted by Arthur DeTore, 11, and Michael DiGregorio, 14. The first scene is a graveyard with the names of important people, including the names of the film-makers, on the gravestones. A tiny bat in the distance flies toward the camera (a series of eight progressively larger cutouts were used), until the bat's face fills the whole screen. Then the bat opens its mouth and inside is the title. The bat flies away. The camera zooms in to a close-up of a tombstone upon which is engraved the name of the film-maker. Then the camera pans over to another tombstone with the names of the assistants.

Film endings can also be very simple, merely showing cutout letters on a colored background, or the ending can be integrated into the film, as was the case in *Smoke! Smoke!*

Another example is provided by the film *Underwater Creatures,* by Paul Falcone. The movie is a ballet of grotesque and beautiful monsters. At the end of the film, all the creatures are defeated by an army, and then sink to the bottom of the ocean. They pile up on top of each other, and one creature opens its mouth to let some bubbles escape. The bubbles drift upward spelling out the words, "The End."

A bat flying toward the camera is the basis of a titling sequence by Steve DeTore, 13. The bat swoops forward until only its face shows, then opens its mouth to reveal the title, $50,000 Per Fang. *Names of the film-maker and his assistants appear on the tombstones.*

Sound

Creating and recording sound to fit the visual images is a very important part of film-making. Some children enjoy this more than any other part of the process. It has a certain immediacy, and it is great fun to make your characters talk on the screen. Atmospheres seem more real with sound.

Adding sound consists of three major tasks. First, there is the creation and recording of the sounds on ¼-inch recording tape. Second, there is the editing of the ¼-inch tape so that the sound synchronizes (coincides) with the picture when the projector and tape recorder are played together. Third, there is the final preparation of sound and picture for a finished print with an optical sound track.

In this section we will deal only with the first two steps, which can be easily done by everyone, using only a projector and a tape recorder. The method described here will enable you to make short films with perfectly synchronized sound. However, you must always use the same equipment to show the films as you used to synchronize them. The steps for making an optical print are explained later in the book, as they are more detailed and greatly increase the cost of your film-making project.

In making animated films, workshop students spend three-fourths of the time on creating the visual portion of the film. They try as much as possible to have the film communicate its ideas without using any sound. The students pretend there will be no sound. The idea is to communicate totally with action. They also try to avoid having a lot of words on the screen, as this can be boring to look at. Then, at the end, when the students have gone as far as they can visually, and the work prints are edited so that every student has his own film just the way he wants it, the class starts on its sound-track sessions.

Everybody works as a group on all of the films in order to make sound tracks. Some students are especially talented in this respect. There have been some films made by the students which were just fair visually, but which came to life with an exciting presence once the sound track was added.

The group works on the sound for one short film at a time. It may take from 15 minutes to 2 hours to create a sound track for an animated film lasting only a minute. The student who made the film prepares a sound-sheet in advance. It lists the different scenes and tells what kind of a sound should be made for each one. The class projects the film and tests the sounds to see if they really fit.

Besides dialogue, other sounds are made vocally. Other sound-making sources are toys and musical instruments, sound-effect records (if the students cannot handle the effect themselves), and—as a last resort—portions of instrumental music on records. It is best for the students to have the experience of creating the whole sound track themselves. However, there is sometimes not enough time, and the class has to resort to records. Sometimes a student has made his film to fit a specific piece of music. When the class does use ready-made music, they try to change it a bit by playing it faster or slower than originally recorded.

◀ *Original musical tracks are used as much as possible. Sisters Amy and Mimi Kravitz combine their talents. Amy, 13, plays the recorder; Mimi, 15, the guitar.*

▲
As Mark Mahoney, 12, awaits his turn, Paul Falcone, 10, and Jean Falcone, 8, use musical instruments and toys to record sounds for an animated movie.

The ideal physical setup for making a sound track is to have the projector in one room, beaming the film through a glass window into an adjoining room, where the students record the sounds. This would keep the sound of the projector motor off the ¼-inch sound tape and enable the students to view the film at the same time they create the sounds. Thus the sounds would be in synchronization with the picture. This would save hours of work later in editing the sound so it is synchronized with the visual images. Unfortunately, this setup is almost never available. The class is usually lucky to find just a simple room away from the sounds of people, typewriters, bands rehearsing, printing presses going, and excessively loud heating or air-conditioning systems.

Most of the time the only alternative is to have the projector in the same room with the tape recorder. The film is projected one scene at a time. The sounds are made while watching the picture, but are not recorded simultaneously. Instead, the projector is turned off and the students record the sounds without watching the film. Sometimes the students get the sound right the first time, but often they make four or five takes in order to get just the right timing and emotional quality in the sound.

Everybody works together, contributing ideas, and the students work themselves up to the mood of the film. There is always a lot of laughing during sound tracks. For the film *Move, Kid,* all of Kathy Ahern's classmates helped with the sound track. Each person in the class played the part of the different people who were telling the boy to "move!" The class needed a rough, male voice for the runner who overtakes the boy on the sidewalk and knocks him into the street. Our two oldest boys had gone home. The younger boys' voices were too high. Finally Debbi Kravitz, 18, grabbed the microphone. She pounded her feet up and down on the floor to simulate running. She panted like a runner and then rasped, "Move, kid . . . argh!" in the coarsest voice imaginable. The whole class split up, collapsing to the floor in laughter. The sight of Debbi jogging up and down with a fierce look on her face was just too much.

Some of the students have specialities. Carol Sones, 17, who created *Just a Fishment of My Imagination,* plays the sexy female voice in the film and is also a "super" old lady. She is the voice of the old-lady neighbor of the motorcycle rider in *Charlie and His Harley,* by Mark Mahoney, 12. Conversing with his mother, she says in a quavery voice, "I saw that motorcycle your son bought, and I hope it won't be a menace to the community!" The mother (also a great old lady by Carol Safton, 14) answers, "Oh, no, he's upstairs doing his geometry." At that point, their conversation is interrupted by a huge roar as Charlie pulls out of the garage on his motorcycle.

Carol Sones is also the voice of the menacing old lady in

Plague, by Amy Schwartz, 15. This is a terrifying, pixillated film about an old witch (a three-dimensional character) who lives in a drab room and wants to maintain the status quo. Some young people (live actors) dance into her room with some windows to let in the sunshine.

The old lady growls, "Who's that coming into my room? Can't you leave anything the way it is! You should be carrying guns instead of windows!"

Then there is a blinding flash like an explosion, which is combined with the sound of a clock ticking to indicate the passage of time. When we next see the scene, the young people have been transformed into old people just like the old lady, except they are life-size, flat cutouts mashed into the wall. The old lady says, "That's better!" In a vicious, crackling voice. Carol continued with a long, impressive monologue, but much of it had to be discarded because the film wasn't long enough.

Another talented sound-track student is Mimi Kravitz, 15. In addition to being witty and capable of many different voices, she also plays the guitar, the piano and various other instruments. She has composed and performed the music for many of our films. The terrific guitar music in *Hair,* a pixillated film by Ellen Richstein, 14, was created and played on the spot by Mimi. She composed and played the piano music for her own animated film *The Tree,* and used a flute and other exotic musical instruments in her other films: *Forgotten War, That's Progress, A Stag Film, Wanderer,* and *Eagle.*

On the first day a sound track is made, the instructor and students should bring all the sound-producing toys and simple tools possible. Also bring musical instruments. The recording equipment should be stored in the studio or workroom. Our staff has used two basic tape recorders to record the sounds with. One is a Sony 200, a four-track machine costing about $200. The other is a Sony 800. This is a smaller, two-track

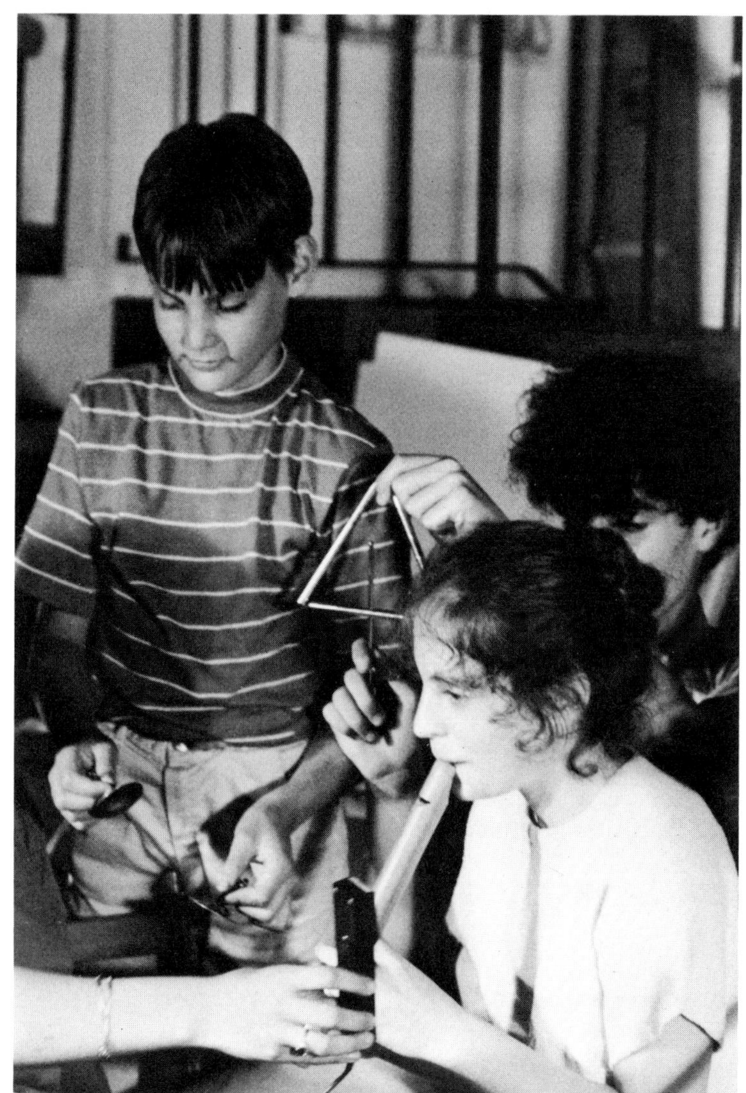

Sound is recorded as Billy Fuchs, 11, plays a set of tiny cymbals, Mark Winer, 17, plays a triangle, and Amy Kravitz plays a flute-like recorder. ▶

▲
The Sony 200 can be stopped and restarted during playback without loss of sound quality. This makes it ideal for editing the 1/4-inch tape.

machine which can be plugged in or battery-run. It has a very good sound quality and is designed to run at a constant 7½ inches per second (ips).

This smaller recorder also costs about $200. We have been using it more and more to record the initial tape, but it is not useful for editing because it is designed for continuous recording. Even after the motor has been warmed up, the machine has to run a little while each time it is stopped in order for it to record or play black well. This makes it inadequate for rapid stopping and starting. The Sony 200 is used for editing. (Sony has replaced the 200 model with the TC 230.)

For playing records, we have a KLH #26 phonograph costing about $250. This machine has a high-quality sound and offers us the advantage of being able to plug in a jack directly from it to either Sony tape recorder. A tape of a phonograph record has a higher quality if you jack it directly from machine to machine. Also, since you are not recording through the air, you can talk or allow noise during this.

We use mostly Scotch brand #111 acetate-base recording tape. This is a good quality, medium-priced tape. Some tapes stretch and your sounds are no longer in synch the day after you have made them. In order to reduce this mishap as much as possible, take several precautions:

(1) Use acetate-base tape, which is supposed to break under strain instead of stretching. A broken tape can be spliced; a stretched tape ruins the synch.

(2) Play the tape through a tape recorder once before actually using it. Hopefully, any stretching that occurs will do so then, before sound is recorded on the tape.

(3) Never rewind recorded tape until just before you are ready to play it. When a tape rewinds on a tape recorder, the action is fast and tight. The tape might sit in this tightly stretched condition for hours, weeks or years, and will get a little out of shape.

(4) Always use new tapes and record only on one side. The use of previously recorded tapes, which could have sounds buried on any of four tracks, could give you a lot of trouble and cost a lot of money if you are going to make an optical sound track for a film.

When recording the sounds, work from a large table that has been covered with a blanket to help soften extra sounds. Put all the sound-effects instruments and the tape recorders on this table. The room must be very quiet. If there is a little echo, hang up a few blankets to absorb the sound.

Assign one student to operate the tape recorder. He must record sounds of good quality. The spoken words must be clearly audible. It is a good idea to have a floor-model stand for your microphone if possible. Then nobody has to hold it. Sometimes if the person holding a microphone wiggles it too much during recording, the result is a crackling noise. Following the recording of each sound sequence, play it back to check the quality and to see if it fits the mood of the film. Assign another student to operate the projector and show the film sequence along with the tape-recorded sound.

Editing and Synchronizing a 1/4-inch Sound Track

In most cases, the class records about 30 minutes of sound for a 60-second film. The student whose film it is must then make a rough edit of this sound, cutting it down to about 5 or 6 minutes. This means that he must play the sounds, pick out the best one or two takes of each effect, and splice the taped sounds together in order. The parts of the tape with the desired sounds are cut out and hung up by attaching the head, or start of the sound, to the edge of the worktable with masking tape, and dropping the tail in a paper bag. The extra taped sounds are thrown away. With only one or two tape recorders available to be used for this editing, the student must often do this work outside of regularly scheduled class hours.

▲
Carol Sones, 17, cuts the portions of sound tape to be used and attaches each piece to the worktable with the ends falling into a paper bag to keep them dirt-free. The projector is set up for use in final "tight" synchronization of sound and picture.

This work tries the patience of some of the younger students. They must have rather close supervision and instruction about just where to cut the tape, so that they do not cut words in half. Remove the dust shield from in front of the magnetic sound head on the tape recorder. Inform the students that the sound is heard when it passes this head. Therefore, if they want to make a cut, it must be done on the right side of the head, either just before the sound is played or just after it is finished.

Once the desired parts of the tape are cut, the next step is to splice all these taped sounds together in the right sequence with about 3 or 4 feet of white leader in the front of the collection and the same amount at the end. This work is played onto a 3-inch reel. It may take the student from 30 minutes to 6 hours to rough-edit the sound track, depending on the length of his film and the types of sounds.

▲
The sound must be cut on the right side of the recorder's magnetic sound head either just before it is heard (as pictured here) or just after it is finished. White tape in picture is leader; brown tape is beginning of sound.

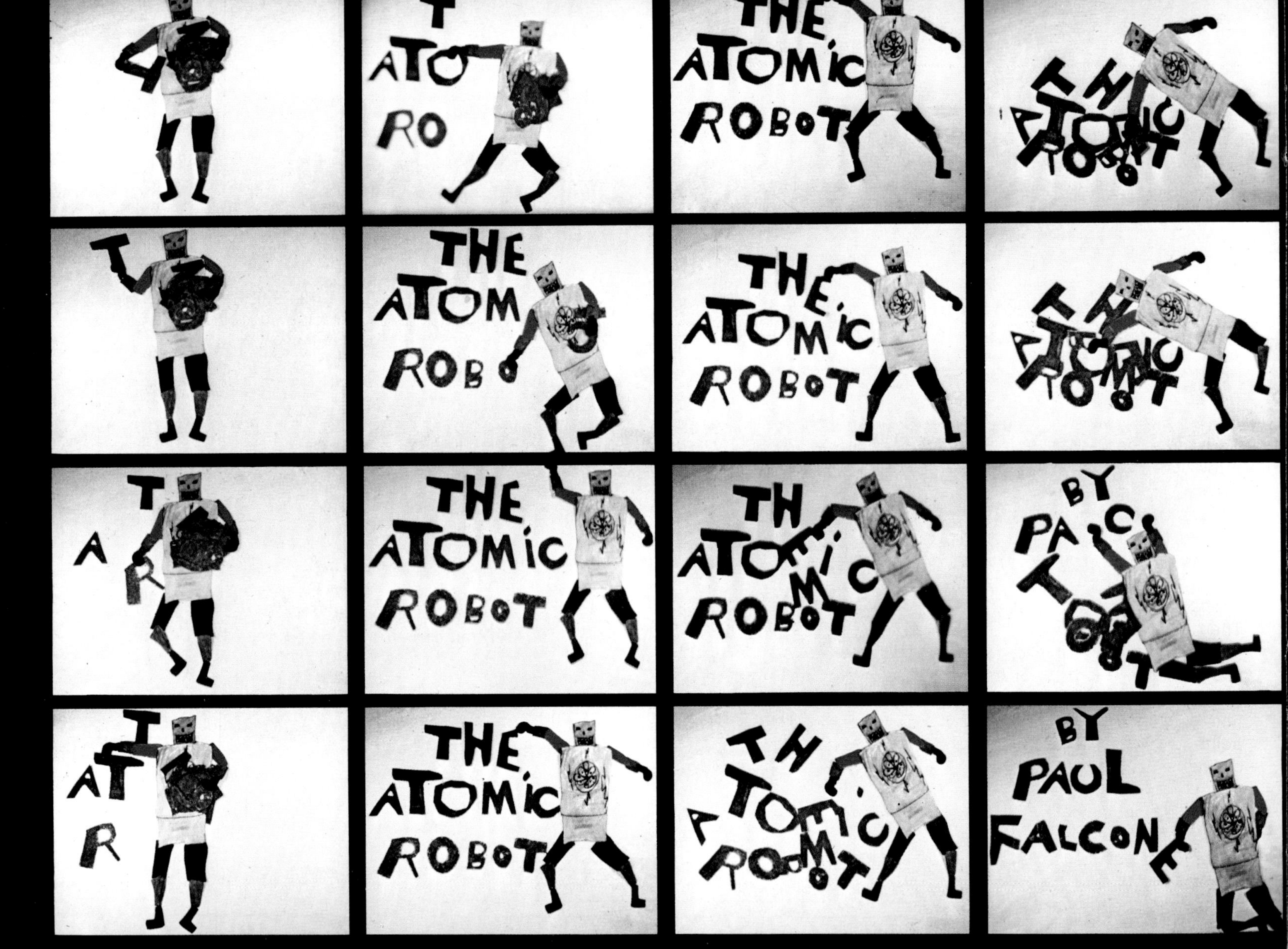
THE ATOMIC ROBOT
BY PAUL FALCONE

Each student works with a very good tape splicer, costing about $1.75, a scissors, a roll of splicing tape, a white grease pencil to mark crucial spots on the sound tape, and a roll of white tape leader.

After this rough edit is done, only second- or third-year students make the final tight edit and synch the sound with the picture. The instructors do this for the younger or first-year students. This tight edit is done by one person at a time, working with the same projector and the same tape recorder to be used for showing the film.

In making this tight synch, the film is loaded onto the projector. The tape is loaded into the tape recorder, with the place where the white leader meets the first sound positioned just in front of the sound head. The projector is turned on. The second the first picture appears, the sound is released. When the picture for that sound ends, the sound must be stopped instantly. The sound tape is cut at this point, and the extra sound is thrown away. If the sound is music and it would cut into a phrase to stop so fast, you could start playing the sound before the picture starts. A way of marking this spot is to punch a small hole in the black film leader at a point shortly before the first picture appears. You would start the sound as soon as you see this punched hole.

The second sound is spliced onto the end of the first sound. Then you must rewind both sound and picture back to the beginning and start all over again. If you have a long film with many effects, it is a lot of trouble to always return to the beginning to keep sound and picture in synch. In this case, you might find a good synch point halfway in the film and return to this point in working with the second half of the film. The entire task of final synchronization will take from 30 minutes to 4 hours, depending on the length of film and type of sound. When you are finished, you have a perfectly synchronized sound and picture—so long as you always show it on the same two machines.

For 16mm film, the best way to always keep sound and picture in synch is to have them converted to a print with an optical sound track. This film can then be shown on any 16mm sound projector, and the sound will always occur at the same points. This process is described later in the book.

For 8mm and Super 8mm film, where optical sound is available but not yet standardized and does not give as good results as 16mm, you can transfer the sound from the ¼-inch tape directly onto a magnetic stripe running the length of the film by using a projector with a magnetic sound head. The tape recorder output is jacked directly into the projector, and the sound head transfers the taped sound. When the projector shows the film, the sound head plays back the magnetic stripe. The sound should precede its corresponding image by 56 frames in 8mm and by 18 frames in Super 8mm for proper synchronization.

◀ *The titling sequence from* The Atomic Robot, *by Paul Falcone, then 8, illustrates how this part of the film can be a dynamic, integral part of it, setting the mood for the viewer. The letters spelling the title and credits are put up in a staccato, robot-like way by the robot himself.*

Photographs and instructions on how to splice recording tape are shown on the following two pages. ▶

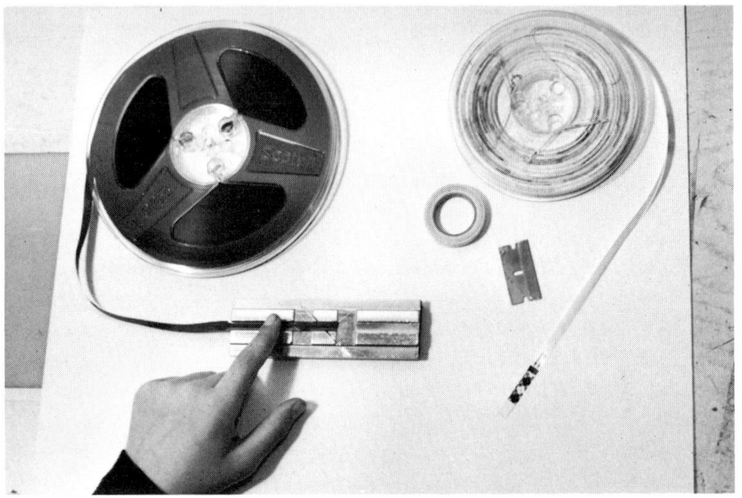

1 *Splicing the portions of tape together is relatively simple. You follow the same directions given here for the pictures showing 1/4-inch white leader being spliced to the front of the sound. Begin by pressing the sound tape, base side up, into the groove of the splicer so it slightly overlaps the diagonal cutting guide.*

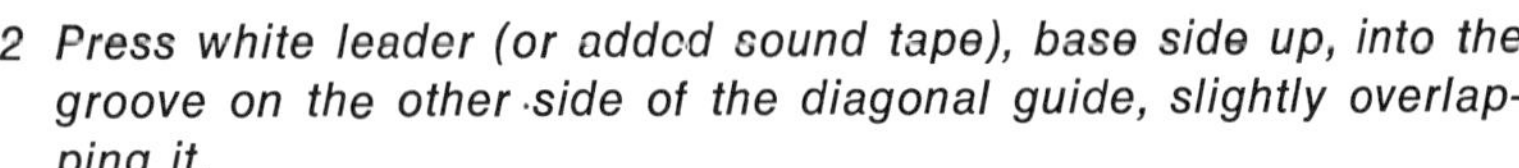

2 *Press white leader (or added sound tape), base side up, into the groove on the other side of the diagonal guide, slightly overlapping it.*

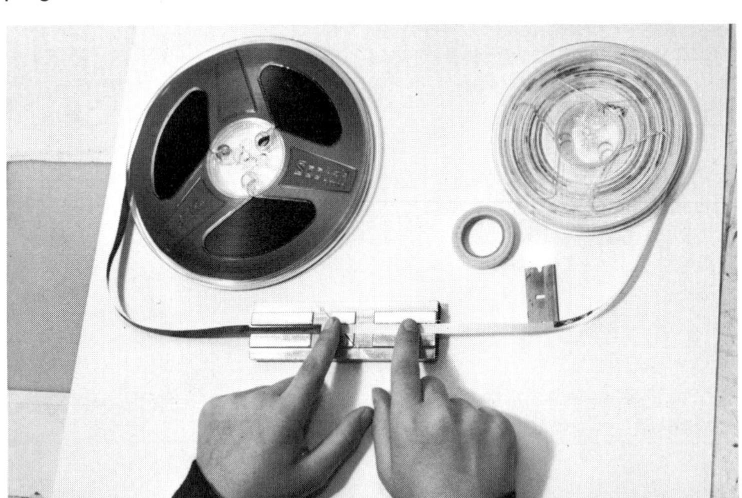

3 *Cut across the tape and the leader (or other tape) with a single-edged razor, following the diagonal guideline.*

4 *Flick off the loose piece of leader (or tape) overlapping the bottom layer of tape. This leaves a smooth surface with the two cut ends meeting at an angle.*

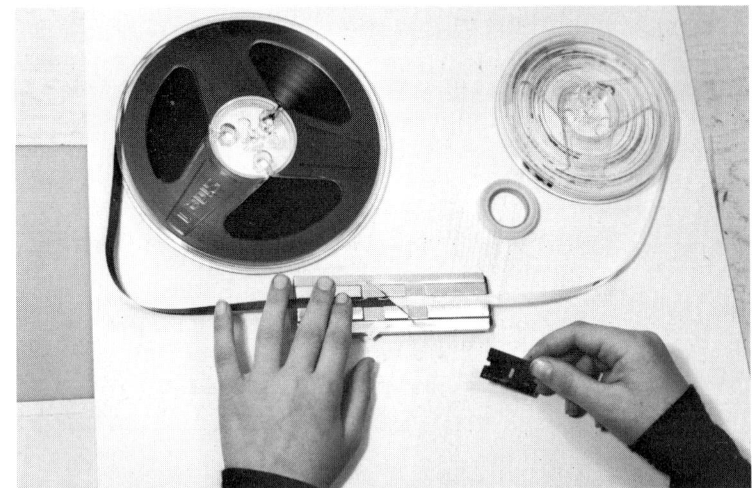

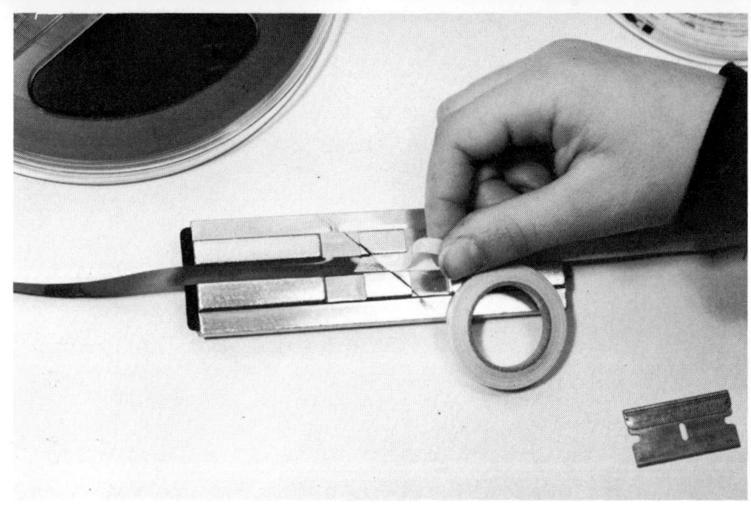

5 *Press a piece of splicing tape across the diagonal line to cover both parts of the joint.*

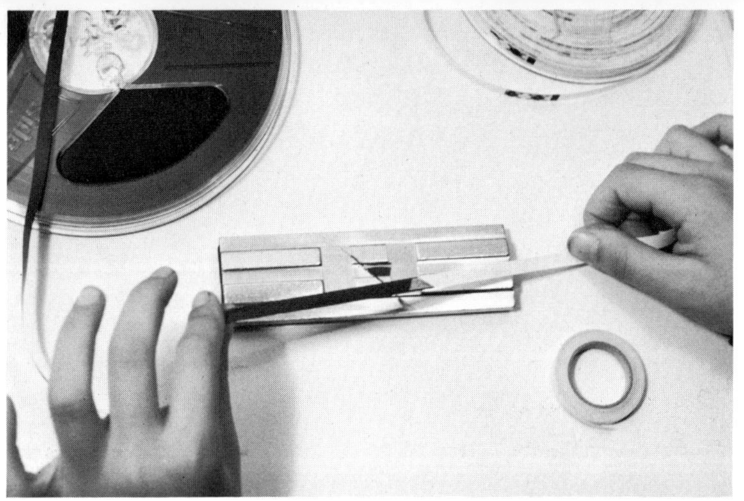

7 *Pull the joined pieces out of the splicer's groove and you have a finished splice. Tape is applied to one side only on all magnetic sound tape.*

6 *Cut off extra splicing tape with a pair of scissors.*

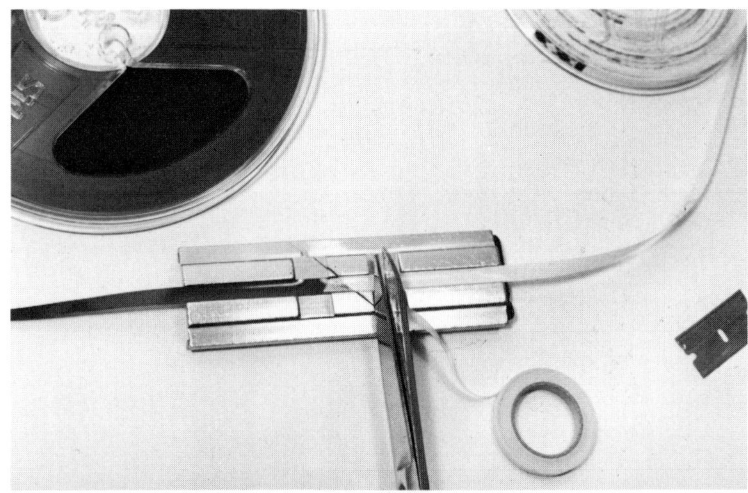

Other Animation with Drawings

Flip Cards

Flip-card films are made by drawing on small, plain 4-by-6-inch white index cards. Each drawing shows the character in a slightly different position with the action a little more advanced. These cards are placed under the camera, one at a time, and filmed for two frames each. The result will be a surprisingly effective piece of animation. The character will have a quivery, alive movement.

There are a number of ways of working. One is with the index cards. In this case, some students like to use an illuminated, glass-topped box to trace the successive drawings, making subtle changes from drawing to drawing. Others prefer to work more roughly, without using a tracing mechanism. They make their series of drawings by just estimating the position of the previous drawing. Some of these students use felt-tipped markers or Cray-Pas crayons for color.

The method our students use most frequently is the scratch-pad technique, using 4-by-6-inch white scratch paper which comes in pads at 10 cents per pad. These can be bought at any stationery store. This paper is so thin that you can see through it. Students often work with ball-point pens or thin-tipped felt markers. In making drawings on these pads or cards, you must keep all the important action in the center of the page. The 4-by-6-inch size is a little too wide even for the wide-angle camera lens. The camera will take an area closer to 4 inches by 5 inches.

◀ *To examine the results of his drawings on 35mm film, Bruce Miller, 12, uses a 35mm film viewer. Film will be reduced to 16mm by a laboratory for projection.*

The slightly larger scratch pads can be cut to the correct size in advance, but that is a lot of trouble.

A lot of drawings are required to get a flip-card film of any length, so the drawings should be kept simple. The flip-card film of two cars colliding is titled *Look Out!* Peter Finklestein, 12, drew the entire sequence on a scratch pad with a ball-point pen in about 30 minutes. To conserve space here, there are about three drawings left out between each one shown. Even so, the action is clear. The two cars meet head on and the occupants are thrown out, moving closer and closer to the camera as they fall. (See page 82.)

The more color that is used in a flip-card film, the longer it takes to complete. Of course, it also usually gets more beautiful. There are different techniques for extending the action without making so many drawings. One is to film each card for more than two frames. The cards can be filmed for four, or eight, or more frames. This causes the film to lose the quivery feeling and assume a more dramatic beat. The action pauses, then moves forward, pauses and then moves forward.

Another technique is to film action in one direction and then refilm the same drawings in the opposite action. An example of this would be a flower growing up and opening its petals. The drawings are made and are filmed in this order. They are then filmed in reverse order so that the flower closes its petals and goes back into the ground.

A student once made four very complex drawings of four dancers. At that point, her patience gave out and she could not make more. We filmed these four drawings over and over and

▲
Animated films using flip cards are inexpensive and require little equipment. Look Out! *by Peter Finklestein, 12, is a sequence of ball-point sketches on a scratch pad.*

extended the dance for a long time.

In filming titles, you must remember that the audience needs 24 frames to read each word. If you want to retain the quivery look in the title without having to make so many drawings, you can make two title cards with a slight difference between them, and film them in alternation every two frames.

Flip cards are inexpensive to make, require little storage room, and can be worked on at almost any time. The technique is especially useful when there are many students and limited access to a camera. Since there is no real animation or manipulation under the camera, very little time is spent in filming. Using a black background, you lay one card down on it and draw a pencil line around the edges. This marks the position where the next cards will be placed to be filmed.

If your camera will not focus on art work this close to the lens,

▲
The Martians Are Coming, *by Paul Falcone, 10, shows a face in various stages of distortion. Each phase was drawn separately.*

▲
The Hit, *by Anthony Schreiner, 12, has a series of pencil drawings in which the pitcher winds up and throws the ball.*

you can purchase an inexpensive close-up lens and an adapter ring to hold it onto the camera lens. This investment will cost you about $6. For extreme close-ups on the workshop's 16mm Bolex reflex camera, we use a Tiffen Photar Plus 3, series #5 close-up lens, which is screwed onto the wide-angle lens with a Tiffen adapter ring, series #5.

Drawing Directly on Film

Drawing on film is the quickest and least expensive way to make a movie. You don't use a camera. You draw directly onto leader film. As soon as the inks are dry, the film is loaded onto a projector and shown. There are several different types of leader which can be drawn or scratched on.

When working on 8mm or Super 8mm white leader, draw with thin felt-tipped markers, or paint with Pelikan drawing inks, type T, especially made for film. Because the film size is so small, most of these efforts will be abstract designs. Lay out a length of the film and have the students decorate it as if it were a ribbon, without any regard for specific frames or pictures. The marker inks dry in about 5 minutes. The Pelikan inks are stronger and more beautiful, but they take about 15 minutes to dry. The colors will take better on the emulsion side of the film. Determine the emulsion side by applying a test swatch of color. The color will bubble on the wrong side. When an abstract film is projected it looks like a show of varicolored lights.

Different work can be done on 16mm clear leader ($3 per 100 feet) and 16mm black leader ($2 per 100 feet). The frame size is four times larger than that in 8mm, and you can draw specific images. In drawing, use flexible crow-quill pen points and thin watercolor brushes, such as Winsor & Newton series 7 brushes, size #0. Images can also be made by scratching on black leader.

The black leader is actually clear leader with a black coating (emulsion) on one side. Where you scratch off this black emulsion, a white line appears. This white line can also be filled in with color. Anything that scratches can be used to make these

▲
Andrea Dietrich, 14, paints directly on 35mm clear leader film with Pelikan ink. The larger film permits greater detail than 16mm allows.

lines. An excellent tool is a line cutter made for silk-screen film. This is a plastic handle with a round, wire loop at the end. It scratches a line and pulls out the emulsion. A single-edged razor blade can also be used. If the black leader is wet, the emulsion comes off more easily.

The film *Fish* was drawn and scratched on clear 16mm leader. First we see the word. It bunches together into the image of a fish. The fish swims across the scene, opening his mouth to exhale some bubbles. He swims through some seaweed, then up to the surface. He pops out of the water into the air and splashes back into the water again.

Because of the limitation of space here, each frame represents about four frames of the actual film. In the title frames, the entire area was painted with blue ink. When the ink was dry, the word was scratched into it. The changing letter-forms and the fish in the next two frames were also scratched in.

The next strip shows the fish moving across the scene. First the fish was drawn by outlining it in black ink. When this was dry, the blue background was painted in. On the third strip, the red seaweed was painted in first; then the fish was outlined in black, and the background was filled in. The fish jumping out of the water (fourth strip) and jumping back in (fifth strip) was outlined before the blue water was added. The unpainted portion in the last strip represents the sky.

The important thing to remember in drawing specific images is that the picture area is between the perforations. Also remember that it takes 24 frames or pictures to make one second of movie (if you project it at sound speed).

One group method is to have a long table, lay out a length of leader and assign each student a single foot of film to decorate. When the whole film is dry, wind it onto a reel and run it on the projector. If the leader used is perforated on both sides, either a sound or silent projector is appropriate. A sound projector must be used if the leader has sprocket holes on only one side, as does film with an optical or a magnetic sound track. Playing music to accompany the film really makes the results seem professional.

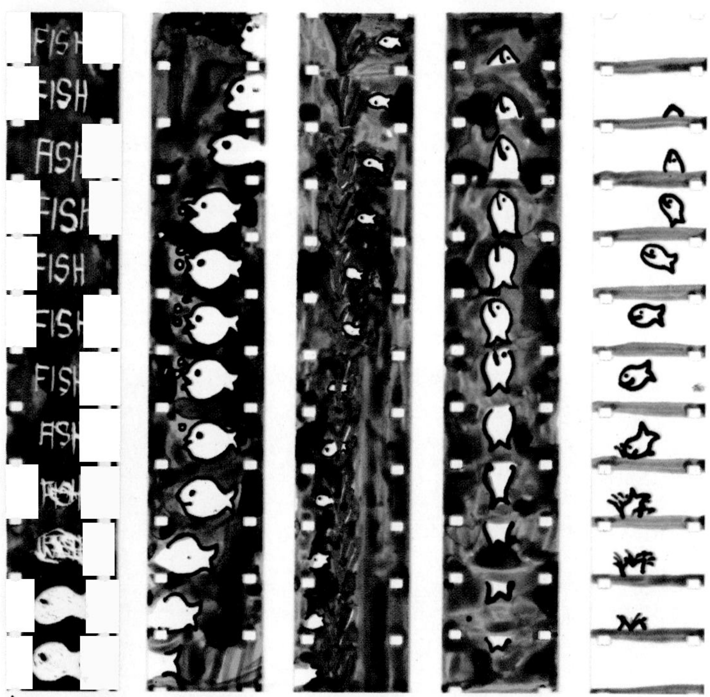

▲
Fish, *by the author, was drawn with colored ink on 16mm clear leader film. The segments shown are cut from the original, which runs in a loop to show the fish swimming through the water, then through seaweed, and leaping upward into the air before returning to the water.*

Using an individual approach to this technique, cut the leader into strips about 7 feet long and give one to each student. When the student is finished, splice the two ends of the film together so that the film forms a loop. Load this loop onto the projector (manual-threading type) and it will run continuously over and over without rethreading. The *Fish* film shown and described is a loop.

Drawing on 35mm film, which is four times the size of 16mm film, should enable students to make more specific drawings. Such work on this size film is now experimental. This 35mm clear leader costs $17 per 1,000 feet. The inks work well on it, but the felt-tipped pens do not. Our group recently bought a simplified 35mm viewer and intends to get a splicer. To eliminate the need for a 35mm projector, after the film is drawn, it will be sent to a lab to have a 16mm reduction print made. The reduction print can then be shown on the 16mm projector. This new technique should give students the freedom of creating animated motion pictures by drawing directly on the film instead of by using the camera to record the art.

Three-Dimensional Animation

The Garden of Eden shown in the film *Eden* is a beautiful place. The opening scene features an iron gate connecting two stone walls. The sign on the gate reads, "Eden." The sign dissolves into another sign which reads, "As Retold by Amy Kravitz." This sign melts away and the gate creaks open, inviting the observer to enter.

Once inside, the camera focuses on a microcosm of the beauties of nature. A tree grows up through brilliantly colored grass. Each blade is a different color. Near the tree grows a daisy. A yellow butterfly flutters in and lands on it; then flies away. The camera moves even closer. The blades of the brilliantly colored grass are enormous in the camera viewfinder. A black spider weaves his web between two stalks of grass. The camera shifts to a tree where white, cotton birds with pink beaks flutter. One by one, the birds fly off the branches.

Suddenly, a swirling black mass at the bottom of the picture parts to reveal a snake. The snake wiggles forward, opening and closing his mouth. He hunches up and down, moving through the grass toward a gnarled, brown tree. Growing on the tree are a number of beautiful, red apples. The snake coils around the tree until it reaches the top branches. At this point, he opens his mouth and issues the invitation, "Take one."

A hand reaches into the scene and takes away an apple. The snake smiles. There is a thunderous voice which warns, "That is a *no-no!*" The camera then cuts back to the gates of Eden.

◀ *The "stars" of* Eden *are two gorillas. Each has a complicated framework covered by a special plaster, clay and fur.*

The apple-eaters are coming out. They are two gorillas. One asks the other, "What do you think, Adam?" Adam answers, "Me like bananas better!" They pause, scratch their heads and bellies, link arms and walk off. "The End," on a red apple, fades out.

All the characters and sets in this film are three-dimensional. The framework of the tree was constructed with cardboard tubing, egg crates, balsa wood, and wire. The framework was then covered over with a material called Pariscraft, which is gauze impregnated with plaster of Paris. When dry, the tree was painted with poster paint. Pariscraft gauze comes in rolls, and is cut into strips, which are dipped into water and applied in very much the same way as papier-mâché.

In the case of the gorillas, each head and body was made of Pariscraft applied around a cardboard shape, with the faces, stomachs, hands, and feet formed of plasteline, a non-hardening clay. Frameworks for the arms and legs were made of thin, flexible, flat metal strips with small holes in them. This is strapping used by plumbers for holding up pipes. The fur was cut from two old hats. For each gorilla, one piece of fur was glued around the head and body. Four pieces were sewn into tubes for the arms and legs and sewn onto the body.

The short blades of grass were long strips of paper colored on both sides with Cray-Pas crayons. One end of each strip was pasted down to a box. The other end was bent up and cut to make a separate blade. The tall stalks used in the spider scene were made of painted paper glued around thin wire which provided support so that they could stand up. The snake was clay wrapped around a wire.

▲
Amy Kravitz outlines the white, paper eyes on her cotton birds, constructed along with other-three dimensional characters and props for her film Eden.

Another three-dimensional construction by Amy is this huge vulture she is painting. The wire and papier-mâché form is hollow and is worn as a costume in the pixillated film War Casualty. ▶

▲
For a close-up scene in Eden, *Amy places a daisy of paper and wire next to a carefully constructed tree trunk.*

There were several difficult animation steps in the film. One was trying to fly the butterfly in to land on the daisy. The plan was to tie clear fishing wire to a balance point on the butterfly's back, but it was simply impossible to balance the butterfly. Finally the butterfly was tied to a stick painted the same color as the sky, and the butterfly was moved into the scene on the stick. Once the butterfly had landed on the daisy, the stick was removed.

Another critical point in filming was the spider spinning his web. The solution was to erect a large sheet of glass, as big as the entire scene, across the middle of the grass stalks and just behind the two large stalks. The wire spider was hung by clear fishing wire from a piece of tape on the top edge of the glass. The spider was gradually inched along and filmed every ¼ of an inch for two frames. The web was drawn on a zigzag course in stages onto the glass behind the spider with a white glass-marking pencil. The total number of frames used to animate the spider weaving his web was 120.

Clay Animation

The workshop students have made a number of animated films with clay figures. One of the first attempts was *Krazy Times,* a 4-minute group effort by seven students, ages 8 to 13. This film was shot in black-and-white Plus-X reversal film. The clay used was gray-green plasteline.

In starting this project, the group made a lot of false assumptions. One was that it would be easy. Another was that the students could make characters and sets at their seats and bring them to the camera ready to film. We had two cameras, and the plan was that one student would cover the total action with a long-shot view, while another would film the important close-up scenes, panning with them as they happened. This would reduce filming time, utilize more students at the cameras, and later give a lot of editing practice.

The students began by making exquisite clay characters. Though they were rather thin, the characters were detailed with pinstriped trousers, polka-dotted coats, etc. We found that when we pressed the characters to make them walk, all the pinstripes disappeared and the thin characters fell over. We concluded that the characters must be mostly rather chunky and simple. Each would take on its own personality by the way its shape changed when it was animated. We found that all the thumbprints in the clay gave a very sensual quality when they were filmed in close-up.

For the sets or backgrounds, the students were given two boards of thin plywood 24 inches by 32 inches. One was covered with clay and used for the ground. The other was covered with clay or painted black and used for the sky. All sorts of trees, bridges, rocks, and other props looked good on the ground, but when the sky portion was placed perpendicular to the ground portion, you could see a hard line where the two boards met. This line was visible even when the bottom board was tilted upward to meet the perpendicular board at a slightly oblique angle. It also seemed to take a long time to get the scenery set up.

The boards had to be firmly braced so that they would not

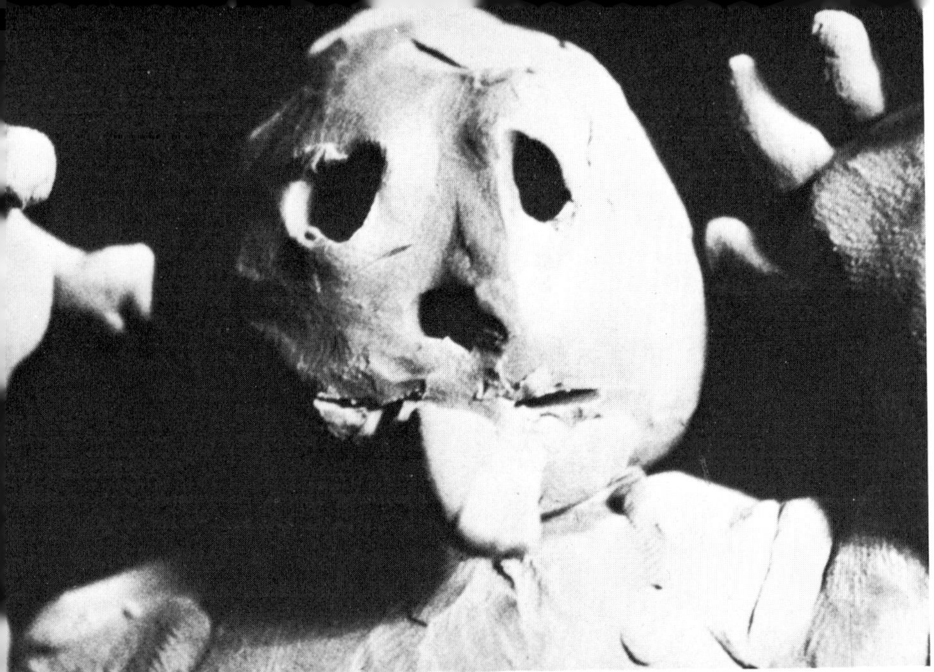

move around when the characters were pressed on them. The line where the boards met had to be gotten rid of by disguising it in some way—usually with bushes. Then we had to determine what the camera angle would be. There was much shifting and tilting up and down of cameras and tripods. Should the shot be from a high angle looking down, or from a low angle looking up?

We had a rough rehearsal of the action of the characters. The clay characters seemed to be like live actors in that they looked better if their faces were kept toward the audience as much as possible. We found problems in lighting and in depth of field (the distances in front of and behind the object in focus at which other images will also be in focus). We had not encountered these problems before in cutout animation, and had not met them to such a degree in three-dimensional animation. In these other types of animation, we had color working for us. Here we had to rely only on light and shadow. Some of our scenes looked washed out, some too contrasty. These had to be done over.

The depth-of-field problem was created by the fact that the lens was set to focus at a particular distance. A few inches in front of that distance would be in focus and so would a few inches in back. The rest would be a little fuzzy. We had to plan where most of the action would be, and focus for that spot. As the character approached this spot from the distance, he might be a little fuzzy; for his main action he would be sharp. When he moved farther toward the camera, he would get fuzzy again. Of course, we could have kept changing focus to follow the character, but this is too difficult for apprentice cameramen.

▲ *Thumbprints left in the clay after the student finishes animating the figure accentuates the character's personality. This close-up is from* Krazy Times; *the figure was done by Paul Falcone, at age 8.*

◀ *Students model their characters with soft, non-hardening clay and film them against a clay background. Figures must be thickset and simplified to withstand handling. These two ladies from* Krazy Times *are by Jane Levy, 10, and Susan Lenk, 10.*

▲ *Diane Gass, 13, sets characters up on a clay background that covers two wooden boards placed so they meet at an approximate right angle. The boards must be braced to prevent movement.*

We found that the shallow depth of field could be used to our advantage. It was quite beautiful and atmospheric to have the character's face sharp and the background fuzzy. Shallow depth of field results from: (a) using a wide aperture, (b) reducing the camera-to-subject distance, or (c) using a telephoto lens rather than a wide-angle or normal focal-length lens. Reversing these factors increases the depth of field.

Another big problem was the close-up camera. It turned out that it was very hard to follow the important close-up action in a pan. The first few attempts were so shaky that we abandoned this technique. The close-up cameraman would wait until the character was going to stand in one spot for a while; then he filmed the close-up.

In time, we decided to try colored-clay animation. Plasticine brand comes in 18 colors. We used about 12 of them, plus the gray plasteline as a base color. This class was held with students ranging in ages from 11 to 17, and most of the students worked on films as one-man projects. We used the two boards for backgrounds again. The ground board was usually covered with a landscape of colored clay formations, but the sky portion was both clay and paint.

Most of the colored clay characters were made in solid sections of color—gray elephants, brown tree trunks, green leaves, etc. But the clay characters in *Magic Mushroom* had white bodies, with areas of mixed colors. Karen Warschaurer, 14, had mixed violet, pink, and blue into swirling colors almost as if she were working with poster paint. One feature of her film we noted with dread. Characters and background were all mostly white; the lack of contrast would make the scene hard to film.

White is always hard to work with in animation. It shows shadows and also makes all your mistakes more visible. Another difficulty in the film was that one of the characters was supposed

◀ *Mead Notkin, 8, works on clay characters and props of different colors for his film* Moon Man.

to fly through the air on a winged creature. Karen had to embed a wired piece of heavy cardboard inside the creature. A length of clear fish wire wrapped around the cardboard and piercing the clay was used to suspend the creature for flight.

These colored clay characters are beautiful to look at in the films, and they have the characteristics of regular clay characters in that they can be bent and twisted, flattened and extended. The disadvantage is that this type of clay seems to get a little brittle when exposed to the air for about six weeks.

Karen is famous for her sound tracks. They are simple narrative stories written and spoken by her. Her first film was *In the Middle* (cutout technique), shown many times on nationwide and local Boston-area television. It is a story of a girl who was too old to do some things and too young for others. "She was too old to cry, and too young to go to a psychiatrist."

Magic Mushroom also has a good sound track. "Once, high up in the sky, there was a sun, and a cloud, and a mother, which meant there were children. . . One day the sun shone between the flowers on the cloud with great care. And so there grew a magic mushroom." (Slide-whistle sound effect as the mushroom grows up.) The mushroom says in a squeaky voice to the family, "Take but one bite from me each and and you will be very happy and know the true meaning of life."

The narrative continues, "So they each took a bite from the magic mushroom. And they were very happy, and knew the true meaning of life. And they all believed they owed it to the magic mushroom, which was in their minds a magnificent mushroom. But, actually, they had always been happy and had known the

◀ *Swirls of colored clay were shaped into a sun that looks down on two of the "people" who live on clouds in the sky. Scene is from* Magic Mushroom, *by Karen Warschauer, 14.*

Mechanical toys are objects that naturally lend themselves to animated film. They can be moved by hand and shot by single-framing, or they can be allowed to run mechanically and be filmed in live action. ▶

BOLEX
H16 Reflex
MADE IN SWITZERLAND
STOP

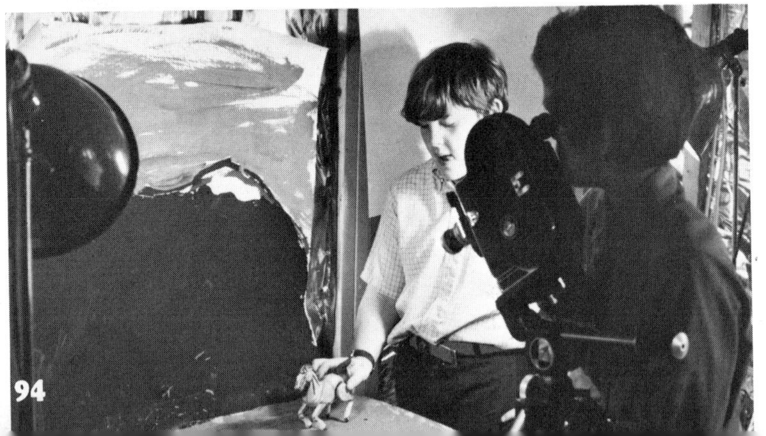

true meaning of life, even though they hadn't realized it." (The mushroom shrinks.) "So who needs a magic mushroom anyway?"

The mushroom grows back up and is shown in an extreme close-up. "You know, I resent that," it says. "You're wrecking my image!" The mushroom holds up a sign saying, "The End."

Toys

Students should experiment with new forms of animation. One such project utilizes toys. Begin by purchasing a dozen small, painted, tin mechanical toys. Have the student wind them up to see what the movements are and then have each child choose a toy to create a film around. It is possible to have one toy used by more than one student, as only two students film at one time.

The students paint scenery for the toys on a wide strip of heavy white paper. The paper is taped into the position it will assume during filming. The sky area is at the top and the ground at the bottom, with the paper curving slightly instead of being perfectly perpendicular at the junction. The single strip of paper eliminates the seam between the sky and the ground.

Students also make props. One prop by David Spence, 13, was a series of cutout snow-covered hills for his toy Santa to ski through. Another was a series of cardboard flowers by Andrea Dietrich, 14, for her string of ladybugs to swarm through.

▲ *Each student creates a setting for the toy he is to film. David Spence, 13, cuts out cardboard props for toy Santa film, while Robert Reiffen, 12, paints his own set.*

▲ *David Spence films his toy Santa against a background of cardboard snowbanks set up in front of the painted snowbanks.*

◀ *Robert Reiffen animates his toy horse while Bruce Miller, 12, films the scene.*

Each student films the total scene in a long shot, in a medium shot, and again in close-up. The results are interesting. Sometimes the mechanical actions of the toys are so hard to control that they have to be animated by hand. Other times, the action is so fascinating that the scene is shot in live action to capture the subtlety of the movements.

The purpose of toy projects is to experiment with the movement of the "found object," and to make new discoveries in the magical world of toys. Another purpose, more closely related to class organization, is to get the students filming and learning camera operation very fast. Painting the sets can take less than one class session, and filming can begin immediately.

Pixillation

Pixillation is filming a live actor as if he were an animated character. In other words, he is single-framed. He is positioned, and a few frames are taken with the camera. Then the actor is repositioned, and a few more frames are taken. The result is a twitchy sort of movement in which the actor resembles an animated character. A special benefit is that the actor can perform improbable feats and interact with inanimate objects.

Pixillation can also add a magical quality to the visual scale. At first sight, the painted set projected on the screen looks as if it might be a small painting. When the actor comes into the scene, the viewer suddenly realizes the enormous size of the set.

This description of the filming might sound as if it would be extremely tedious for the actors to hold their poses for so long, but the actors do not actually hold still. First there is a walk-through rehearsal to see how the actors look in the camera. Then they start their actions in a *continuous slow motion,* while the cameramen click away with their thumbs on the single-frame button. When a cameraman's thumb gets tired, or when an in-

Assistant Carol Sones and student David Lipworth operate the cameras for a pixillated film. ▶

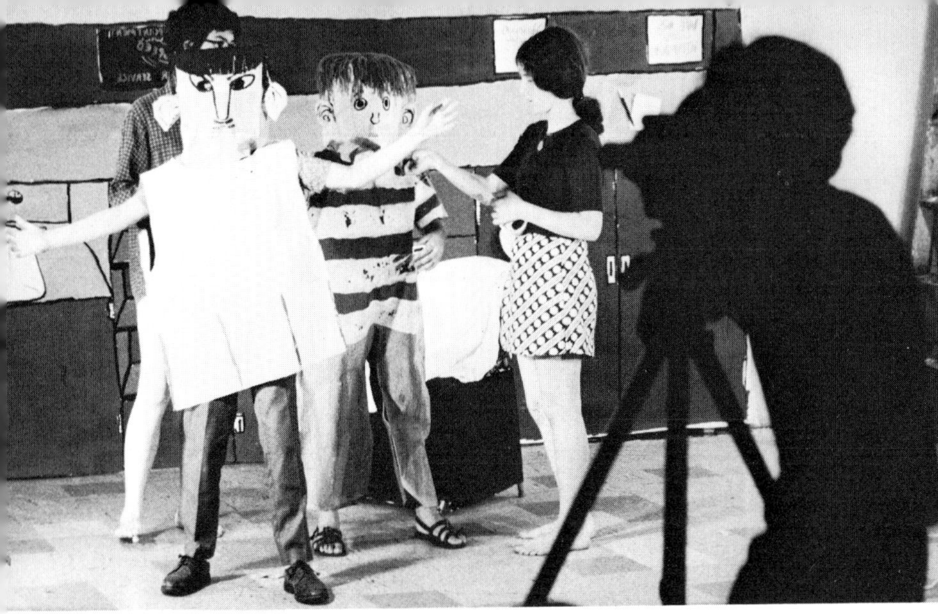

animate object is introduced into the scene for interaction with the actor, the chief cameraman yells, "Freeze!" The actors hold their respective positions, the thumbs get rested, and the assistants run in to start the animation of the props. The faster the single-frame action is, the closer it will resemble live-action movement. The slower it is, the more frantic and bizarre the actors' movements will appear to be on the screen.

Pixillated films are fun because the objects and scenery have been enlarged in size. Of course, you must have a large, permanent place in which to do this work. Besides needing enough room for scenery and props, you need work space for making masks and costumes. A good procedure is to start with masks first. Paper bags that fit over the entire head make excellent masks and can be quickly painted and completed in one class session. The younger students (up to age 13) attack this project with great relish. Older students often prefer to make a more complex head, using chicken wire for the shape with papier-mâché on top. Other students prefer not to make a mask, but to have the character wear make-up and a wig. Have available lots of different-colored, cheap, Halloween wigs for use as hair, beards, moustaches, etc.

The next step is the costume for the body. Basic materials are a large roll of rather wide, brown wrapping paper, scissors, and several hand-gripped staplers. Lay a length of paper out on the floor and fold it in half across the width. The fold is where the head and the shoulders will go. Cut a semicircle from the fold, making a hole for the head to go through. Cut the shoulder parts

▲ *In pixillation, live actors are made to resemble cartoon characters with masks and costumes. As the actors move in continuous slow motion, one or more cameramen film the action by single-framing it. Students here are working on a scene from* Shortcut, *by Rebecca Snider, 14.*

◀ *Rebecca puts a few finishing touches on a one-piece paper costume for one of the actors in* Shortcut. *Mask is a painted paper bag, topped by hair from a Halloween wig.*

of the fold so they are tapered down slightly. Staple the paper together along both shoulders and along the sides of the costume. The result is a long, sleeveless coat which can be shortened, or furnished with sleeves, and painted with poster colors. If the character needs legs, split the coat up the middle, leaving the outer sides stapled together. The inner sides of the legs are not stapled until the actor is inside the costume and ready to be filmed.

Cloth costumes are feasible if the student brings them ready-made, or if they do not require sewing, which takes too much time. In the film *Coffin Child,* by Mark Winer, 17, Dracula wears a velvet cape with his paper head and paper fingernails. His victim is in regular street clothes and wears no mask. In *Kaleidoscope Eyes,* by Liane McKayle, 11, the characters have paper heads and cloth costumes. Liane made their costumes simply by draping lengths of colored cloths around the actors. To complete the costuming, the arms of the actors can be painted appropriately with poster color, or the actor can wear a color-matched sweater under his costume. Hands are usually painted or are covered with cheap, white, paint gloves purchased in the hardware store. These gloves in themselves have a cartoon look.

One student made a costume and head entirely out of chicken wire and papier-mâché. It is a vulture costume in the film *War Casualty,* by Amy Kravitz, 13, (see color picture, page 88). The costume covers the entire body of the actor except for her legs, which were painted to resemble the bird's legs.

Amy Schwartz, 15, made her main character completely out of chicken wire and papier-mâché for her film *Plague.* The character, an old lady, sits in a chair during the film, while live actors move about. Her head can be moved from side to side because it is a hollow, separate piece, attached to the body with a broom handle which runs down through the figure. The eyes and mouth are of colored clay, which is manipulated as the lady talks to the live actors, who have no masks and are dressed in street clothes.

In addition to masks and costumes, you have to create the scenery or set. This consists primarily of a painted backdrop of paper. You can glue together long strips of wrapping paper, but it is easier to purchase tall rolls of heavy white background paper. This paper comes in rolls about 108 inches wide, and costs about $13 per roll. One roll is enough for three different sets. Each set is about 8 feet by 10 feet. Use the best quality poster colors and wide paintbrushes from the hardware store for

Amy Schwartz, 15, animates the clay eyes of her main character, which is constructed of chicken wire and papier-mâché. The flat life-sized figures against the wall have taken the place of the live actors who were filmed by pixillation in the previous scene of her movie Plague.

▼

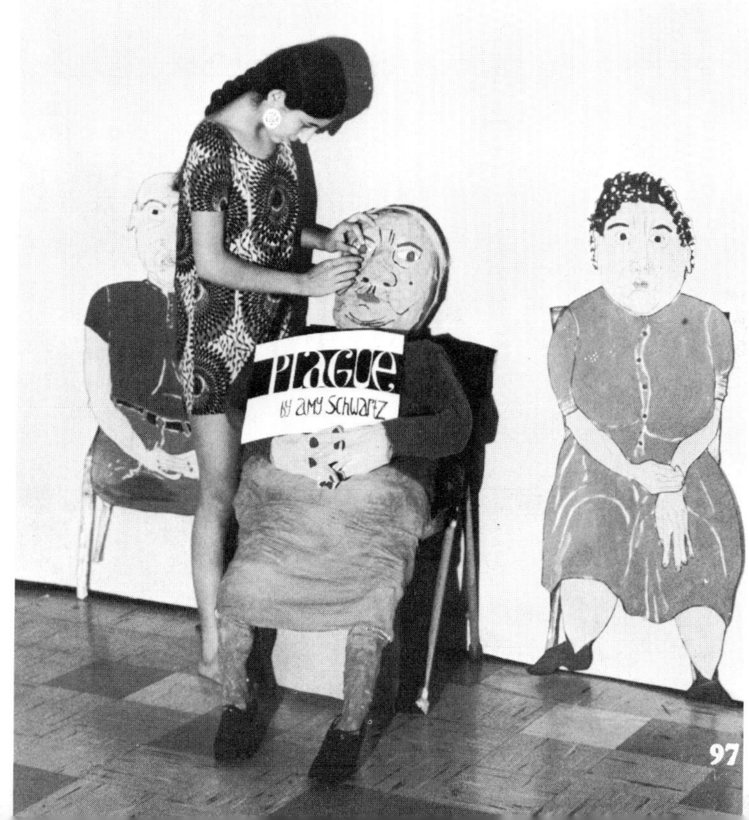

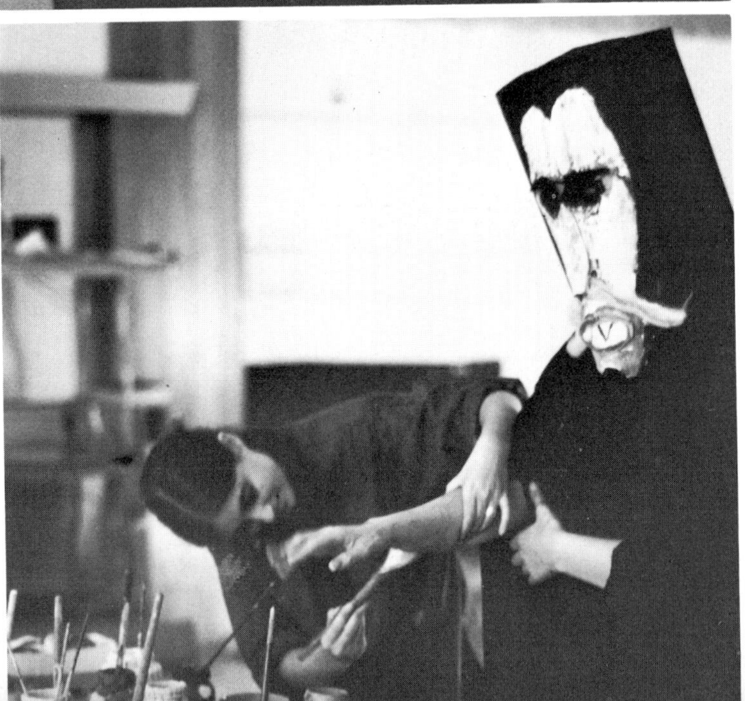

painting the backdrop. Tape a long strip of brown wrapping paper to the floor beneath the backdrop to keep the floor clean from paint drippings. In filming the scenes, try to keep the camera high enough so that you do not see the floor. In some cases, you can film the actual floor as it is.

The final step is to determine what props the character will need to complete the set. One set in *Coffin Child* required a huge coffin. This was fashioned from a flat piece of corrugated cardboard propped up from behind with two chairs. Dracula emerges from the coffin and turns the hinged sign on the coffin. He turns it from the side that reads, "The Count is in!" to the other side, which says, "Out for a bite." Later in the film, the set is used again. The Count then needs additional props—a wine bottle and two glasses—for a party. (In a surprise twist, his intended victim becomes his guest and the two characters have a grand time.)

Besides the coffin set, this film needed another big set—a park. There was a tree with a sign which said, "Keep your park clean." Directly next to the tree was a trash barrel. Its overflowing litter spilled onto the set. Another prop was a park bench on which the "victim" was to sit. The bench was made by covering some chairs with wrapping paper and then painting the paper to look like a park bench. The female victim sits on the bench and reads a magazine labeled *Truest Confessions,* while the Count sneaks up. This scene was filmed at the last minute, when the class was supposed to be over. As the students were filming a close-up on the scene, a well-meaning school janitor walked into the scene and started cleaning up the "trash" on the set.

▲ *Masked actor in a velvet cape plays Count Dracula in* Coffin Child, *film by Mark Winer, 17.*

◀ *Assistant Joanne Ricca paints Dracula's arms and hands with poster color to complete the costuming.*

With the backdrop and the props in place, the camera operators film Dracula emerging from his coffin. ▶

THE COUNT IS IN

Optical Sound

The electrical sound impulses printed as photographic images along the film edge form the optical track. If you want your finished film to have an optical sound track on it, you have to send it to the laboratory. The lab makes an optical image of the sound on clear film, then prints that together with the visual images of the original film. There are two ways of handling optical sound:

(1) You can give the original, edited film (which you have either edited directly or from a work print) and your edited ¼-inch sound tape to your laboratory, and tell them you want a

An optical sound track is made and printed on film to coincide with the picture. The process has many steps. The original, processed film (1) is never run through the projector. Instead, you have a work print (2) made from the original. You use the work print for all editing and sound synchronization. (3) You record the sounds on 1/4-inch sound tape and edit this tape to synchronize with the work print. (4) You send the edited 1/4-inch tape to the laboratory, where it is transferred to this 16mm magnetic tape with sprocket holes. Using a synchronizer, you run this tape and the edited work print through together, matching the sounds and pictures frame by frame. (5) The edited 16mm sound tape goes to the laboratory, where it is transferred as photographic images (appearing as wavy lines) on clear 16mm film. This is the optical sound track. (6) The final film is a composite print of the optical sound and the original 16mm picture (edited by you to match the synchronized work print). This composite is done by the laboratory. ▶

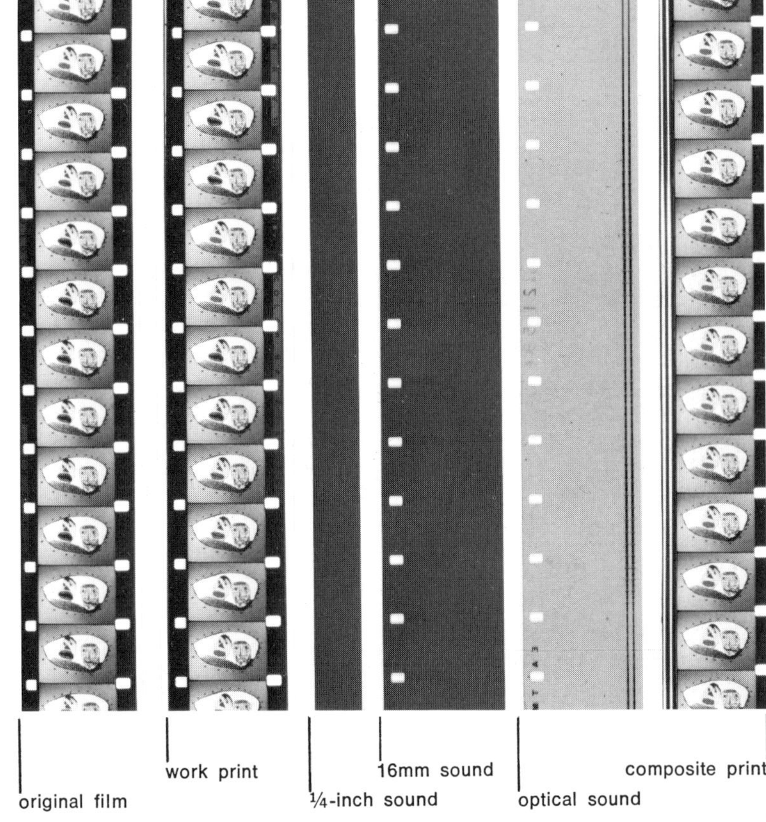

copy of the film with a synchronized optical sound track. You must also give them a sound-sheet which lists each scene and the sound that goes with it. In this case, the lab is doing a lot of sound editing and synchronization, because playback machines differ and the ¼-inch tape usually gets longer than the picture when it is transferred to optical sound. The lab will charge you by the hour for this kind of work, and it is expensive.

(2) Your other choice is to have the ¼-inch sound track transferred to 16mm magnetic tape and then take care of all this re-editing and synchronization yourself. You will need to buy or rent a synchronizer with a magnetic sound head, a sound amplifier to plug the synchronizer's sound head into, a guillotine tape splicer, and a pair of long-shank rewinds with two reels apiece.

The setup for synchronizing the 16mm sound tape and the edited work print consists of a pair of rewinds, four reels, a sound amplifier, and a synchronizer with a magnetic sound head.

At first, it is gratifying to just get a good visual picture and a well-edited ¼-inch sound tape to run with it and to let the laboratory do the rest. But eventually, it is more satisfying to do as much work on the film by yourself as is possible. You always feel that you could have matched the sound and picture just a little better, since you know the film better than the lab does.

The technique employing 16mm sound tape has many steps. To begin, when you have the original film processed, also get either a work print or a timed print (which can be even better in lighting quality than the original). The original is carefully filed away and never run through the projector.

All editing is done on the work print or on the timed copy. Students use this film to learn to load projectors and make

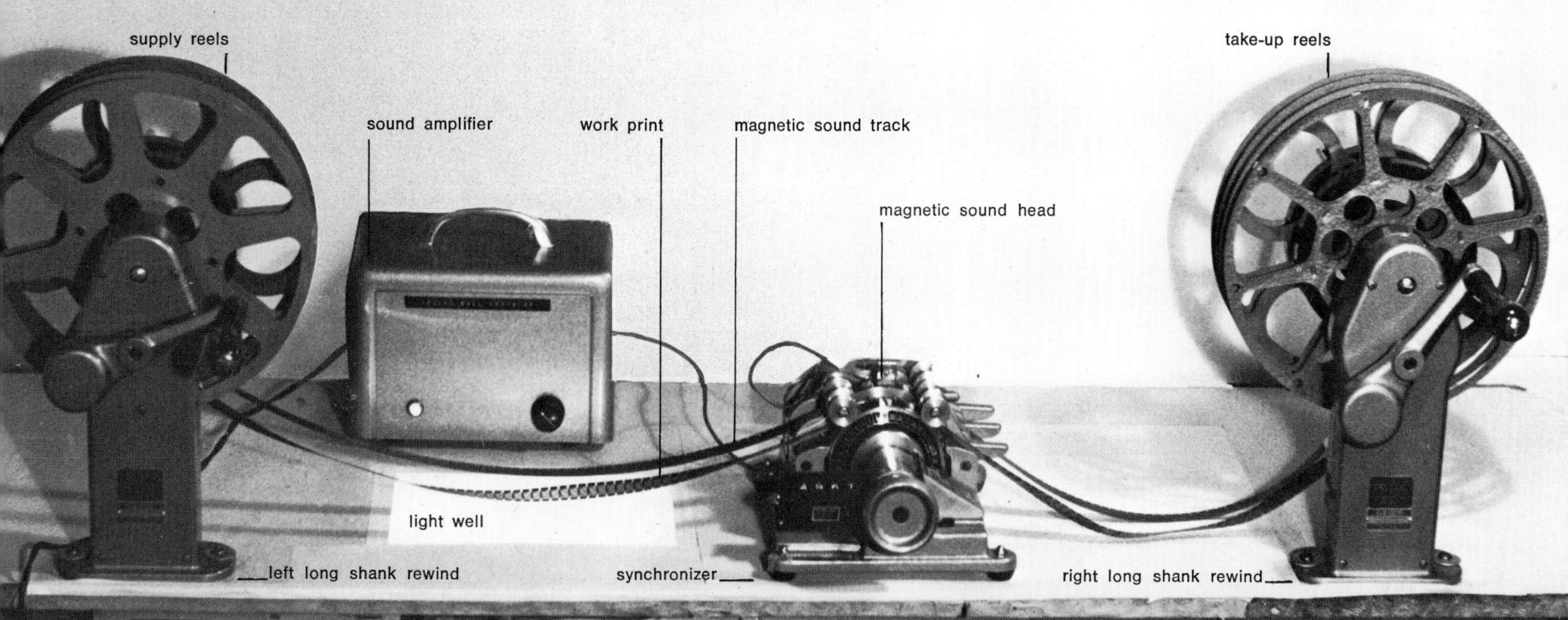

splices. In case of any disaster causing the film to be torn up, the scenes will not have to be refilmed. You can just have another copy made from the original. This work print is edited until it is just the way the student wants it. A ¼-inch sound track is made and edited so that if you always use the same projector and the same tape recorder, they will run in pretty close synch.

This ¼-inch tape is taken to a sound studio or your lab, and transferred to 16mm magnetic sound tape. This new tape of your sound is the same color as regular sound tape, but it is larger, the size of 16mm film, and has sprocket holes along one side. The sound studio or lab will charge you for the raw 16mm tape and for their time in transferring the sound. A rough estimate is that 1,200 feet of stock (raw tape) will cost you about $25, and an hour of lab time may range from $25 to $125. You should shop around for both the price of the transfer and the quality of the work.

Then you return to your workshop and synchronize this new sound so that it fits exactly with your picture (work print). Most of the time, because the speed of the projector or the tape recorders may not have been precise, you will find that the new sound lasts longer than before and does not fit the picture anymore. Small portions of sound have to be cut out of the track to make it fit. This is usually no problem in working with voices or with sound effects. When you run the 16mm sound through the synchronizer, by cranking the rewind, you can hear these sounds clearly, and there are always small, silent spaces in between which can be cut out. The big problem occurs with music. This is hard to hear well on the simple synchronization setup described here. The reason is that the tape cannot be wound through the synchronizer at a constant sound speed. It is therefore hard to hear and cut exact musical phrases. However, it can be done if you have patience.

First, load the 16mm sound tape into the synchronizer under the magnetic sound head. Plug the sound-head cord into the amplifier. As you wind the sound through the synchronizer, the amplifier will play the sound. Run the entire sound track through this system by itself, marking the beginning of each sound on

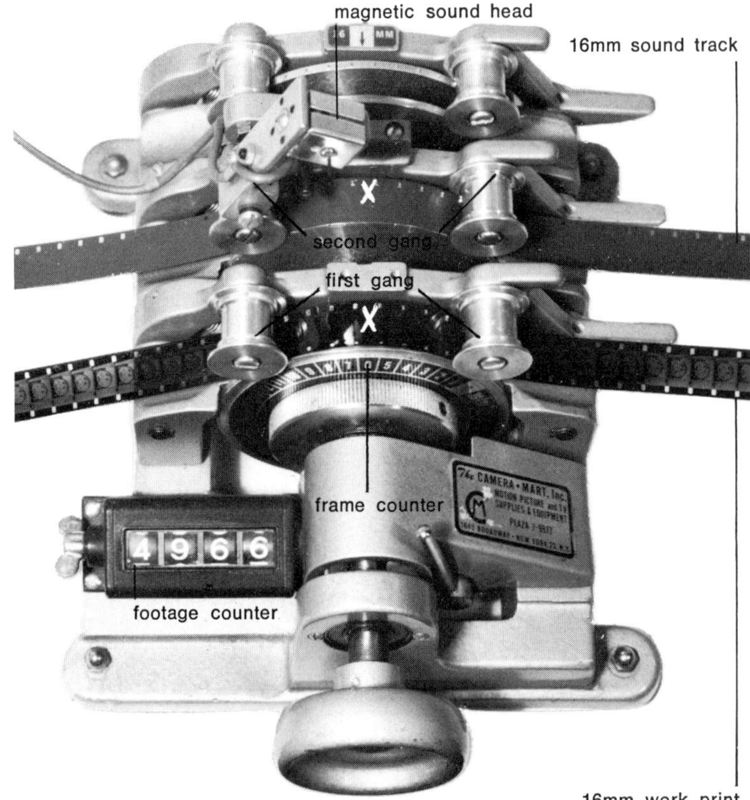

▲
The edited work print is loaded onto the sprockets of the first gang, where it is held in place by the two front rollers. The magnetic sound tape is loaded onto the sprockets of the second gang, which has a magnetic sound head. Sound "X" under the upraised sound head must coincide with the picture ("X") directly below on the front gang.

the tape with a white grease pencil. Check the listing on your sound-sheet and choose labels for specific sounds. For example, a dog barking might be marked "dog"; an explosion, "bomb."

When the sound has been marked, load the picture from the left-hand reel into the front gang (sprocket wheels) of the synchronizer and the sound from the second left-hand reel into the second gang, under the magnetic head. The reels on the left rewind feed through the synchronizer and onto the right-side take-up reels. Each pair of reels on the rewinds are kept apart with special spacers and are held tightly to the long shaft with a spring clamp.

Both sound and picture have leaders on them. The synchronizer has counters to show the number of frames and of feet pulled through. Most of the time, the sound starts exactly when the picture starts.

There are two ways of synchronizing the film and sound. One way is to be sure the correct sound is just under the magnetic head at the same time the exact picture is in line with it on the front synch gang. This method is sometimes useful to line up sound and picture, though the small picture is hard to see.

When using this method of synchronization, mark the picture corresponding to the sound with an "X" or with the same code initials as the sound. Also make a punch mark on the leader 6 feet before the first frame of the picture and on the 16mm magnetic sound tape leader 6 feet before the first sound starts. Thus you end up with sound and picture lined up one above the other in "editing, or level, synch." The laboratory must then pull the whole optical track made from the sound tape forward 26 frames before making a composite print of it and the visual image. This is because when a film runs through a projector the sound head is located 26 frames ahead of the lens.

An alternative method is to incorporate a Moviescop viewer right next to the synchronizer. Set the frame counter on the synchronizer to 26 frames, and put the first frame of the picture over this counter. Then back-wind the picture onto the left-hand rewind until this first picture appears in the Moviescop viewer. The Moviescop viewer should be placed so that when this first

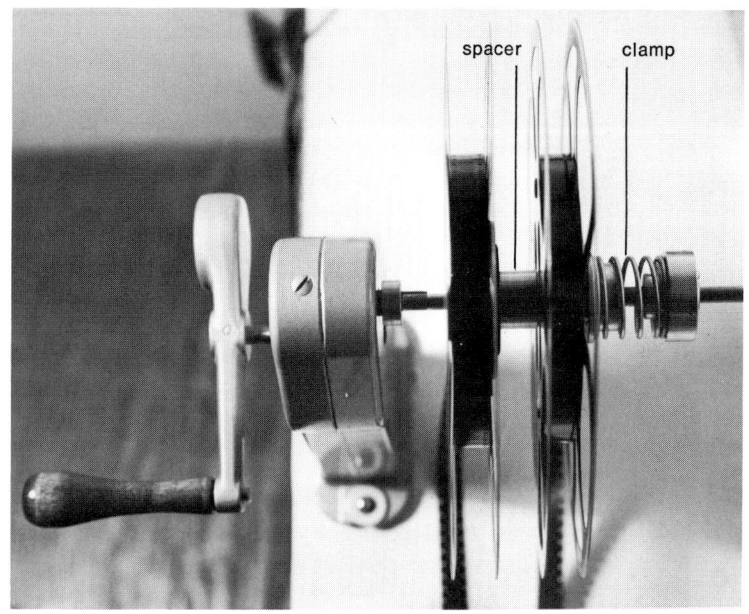

▲
A spacer between the two reels holds them apart, while a spring clamp holds them firmly to the rewind.

picture appears, the frame counter reads 0 and the magnetic head of the synchronizer is over the 0. The exact sound for this picture should then be placed under the magnetic head. Thus the sound will run through the synchronizer and onto the right-hand take-up reel just 26 frames ahead of the picture. You can see the picture in the viewer and hear the corresponding sound at the same time. You will end up with the picture and the sound in "printing synch."

When using this method of synchronization, mark both picture and sound clearly with punch-holes that line up with each other just 6 feet before the first sound starts. That means that the first picture will be 6 feet and 26 frames behind the punch mark. Trans-

fer this punch mark to the original film when you are ready to send it to the lab with the sound tape. Tell the lab that if they match these holes, the picture and sound will be in "printing synch." The lab will replace your punch-hole on the sound with a beep tone.

The next step is to take your original film and synchronize it to fit the edited work print. Each scene must be spliced together carefully so that it corresponds exactly, frame for frame, with the work print. If you are working in animation, the start and stop of the scenes are easy to see. In live action, they are harder. Have edge numbers printed through from the original onto the work print. These numbers are spaced about every 6 inches along the edge of both the original and the work print and are the same. If you match these numbers exactly, the original film will match the work print.

When you are ready to edit your original film, the uncut reels have to be cut apart scene by scene and hung up on a rack. Each strip of film or group of scenes is labeled. Wear cotton

◀ *When a Moviescop viewer is added to the setup, the first frame of the picture is placed on the front gang in line with the magnetic sound head on the second gang, and is then back-wound 26 frames to appear in the viewer. The frame counter should read 0 then, and you can place the start of the sound for that picture under the magnetic head.*

gloves when handling the original film, to protect it from dust and fingerprints. Although you can use tape splices for the work print, and on one side of the magnetic sound, you should use a cement splicer for the original film. When your film is synchronized, you give the lab the original film and the magnetic 16mm sound. The lab converts the magnetic sound to optical sound. The optical track is clear 16mm film with a wavy line running down one side. Your final composite print is made by printing both the original picture and the optical sound onto the same film. You now have a film which can be played on any sound projector and the sounds will always occur at the same place.

In working with children, you should allow them to edit all work prints and ¼-inch tapes. Synchronization of work print with 16mm magnetic sound tape, and of the original film with the work print, should be done by older students, 13 years and up, who are second- or third-year students. Each of these students does the work on his own film only. The instructors have to synchronize the films for the younger or the first-year students. It takes a student two to four hours to match a 16mm magnetic sound tape with the work print for a minute of animated film with about eight scenes and about 20 sound effects. It takes another four hours to synch the original with the work print.

Editing the original film to coincide with the edited work print, Joanne Ricca and Kathy Ahern wear white gloves to protect the film. Each strip is labeled and carefully hung in place for splicing. ▶

How to Adapt Unequipped Movie Cameras

Single Framing

If your camera has no built-in single-frame release, you may be able to purchase an attachment to allow single-framing. However, if an attachment is not available, you can achieve the same effect by just quickly tapping the camera's trigger when you film, so that you take the least number of frames possible.

If your camera has a frames-per-second control, turn this so that you take 8 frames per second or 12 frames per second instead of the customary 16 or 24. This will give you a better chance of taking fewer frames every time you tap the trigger. (When changing the frames per second, do not forget to read your light meter according to that shutter speed instead of 16 fps, or your aperture setting and exposure will be wrong.)

Non-reflex Focusing

Reflex cameras allow you to regulate the focusing by twisting a ring on the camera lens until you obtain a sharp image on the ground glass (or other device) in the viewfinder. (The other devices include either a microprism screen or a split-image screen.) There is also a through-the-lens focusing camera that uses a rangefinder system which allows accurate focusing. However, many cameras have only the distance-setting ring on the lens and no device in the viewer allowing you to see whether or not the image is in focus. For these cameras you must measure the distance from the subject (art work) to the *film plane* (the position of the film behind the lens). Set this distance on the lens' ring, which is marked off in feet. You must be accurate for close-ups. You may need to attach a close-up lens as described next.

Many inexpensive cameras have fixed focusing, which means that everything 6 feet or more beyond the lens will be in focus; anything closer will be out of focus. Some of these cameras can have close-up lens purchased for them. You should take your camera to the store to be fitted for one. This lens may be held onto your camera lens by pressure, or may be screwed on, or may be taped on with masking tape. If the salesman cannot recommend any special lens, you should purchase a Kodak close-up lens and make a test.

Place your camera on a tripod or a titling stand, pointing the lens down at the art work. On one side of the art work, place a card with a big number on it. This number indicates how far away the camera is from the art work. You should start at 8 inches. Film a few feet, then move the camera to 9 inches; place a new, 9-inch card on the art work and film a few more feet. Continue doing this until you reach 2½ feet. Animation done farther away than this is too much trouble. When this film is developed, the number that is clearest alongside the art will tell you how far away the camera should be kept for animation.

If your picture still looks blurry, purchase an extra close-up lens and tape that so it is right over the first one, giving you two extra lenses on the camera. Make your test again with both lenses.

Non-reflex Viewing

Reflex viewing is when the image is transmitted, by mirrors, from the lens to the viewfinder, so that the area you see is exactly the area the camera will film. The effect is the same as it would be if you were actually looking through the lens. On many cameras there is no reflex viewing. Instead, the viewfinder is a separate unit in the camera and is usually to one side of the lens, and a few inches above or below it. This does not affect your picture-taking when you film objects which are at least 6 feet away. However, this small distance between the viewfinder opening and lens opening creates a big problem when filming art work close-up. This problem is called "parallax."

A typical parallax problem can be illustrated by setting up such a camera about 2 feet away from some art work and placing the art so that it appears to be perfectly centered when you look through the viewfinder. Film the art work and have the pictures processed. When your film comes back from the lab, the art work will be over to one side and either too high or too low, with some of it cut off. Half of your film would be a picture of the table the art was on.

You may be able to match your camera with a titling stand that will take art work of a particular size and center it in front of your camera, solving all your parallax problems. If not, you can fasten your camera to a medium-sized, vertical titling stand.

Place the art work on your table and look at it through the viewfinder. Move the camera until the art work looks centered and fills the viewing area of the finder. Then roll a sheet of paper up into a tube and place one end of the tube around the camera's lens. Move the art work until its center is directly under the center of the tube extending from the lens. Even if the picture looks off-center through the viewfinder, it will be taken correctly through the lens. Remember to film the art work against a black background in case you get a few edges.

The techniques outlined in this chapter show that virtually any movie camera can be used for animation, so you need not be limited by your equipment. Hopefully, this fact will encourage you to try out the methods described in this book and to experiment with new ones. Film animation is a very useful tool in many areas. In education, it is used to explain mathematical and scientific concepts which cannot be easily shown by live-action filming. Note, for example, the large amount of animation used on television to depict details of space exploration and the moon landing. Advertising companies use animation in television commercials because it lends itself so well to telling a bold, concise story in a short length of time. Historically, it has been used to entertain children. The Yellow Ball Workshop is now teaching it to children for use as a modern means of artistic expression capable of communicating ideas and feelings to a worldwide audience.

Filmography

The films described in this book are parts of prize-winning reels, which are collections of short films made by students of Yvonne Andersen. The reels are titled:

The Amazing Colossal Man, 1964
The Yellow Ball Cache, 1965
Bag 5, 1966
Cinder City Plus 6, 1966
Menagerie, 1967
The Newton Mini-Films, 1967
Pool, 1968
Rainbow Reel, 1968
Plum Pudding, 1969

Let's Make a Film, a documentary film showing students at work on animated films, was made available in mid-1970.

Illustrations

Project / Student & Age / School*& Year / *Pages*

Camera Operation / Paul Shoul, 11 / NCAC, 1969 / *17*
Editing / Tristian Hickey, 12 / NCAC, 1969 / *20*
Art Work / Jean Falcone, 8 / YBW, 1969 / *24*
Projection / Jean Falcone, 8 / YBW, 1969 / *41*
Editing / Kathy Ahern, 16; Y. Andersen / NCAC, 1969 / *44*
Editing / Amy Kravitz, 13 / NCAC, 1969 / *46*
Sound / Mimi Kravitz, 15 / NCAC, 1969 / *70*
Sound / Amy Kravitz, 13 / NCAC, 1969 / *70, 73*
Sound / Billy Fuchs, 11; Mark Winer, 17 / NCAC, 1969 / *73*
Sound editing / Carol Sones, 17 / YBW, 1970 / *75*
Drawing on film / Bruce Miller, 12 / YBW, 1970 / *80*
Drawing on film / Andrea Dietrich, 14 / YBW, 1970 / *84*
Clay animation / Mead Notkin, 8 / YBW, 1970 / *91*
Clay animation / Diane Gass, 13 / NCAC, 1969 / *91*
Toy animation / David Spence, 13; Robert Reiffen, 12; Bruce Miller, 12 / YBW, 1970 / *94*
Camera Operation / Carol Sones, 17; David Lipworth, 13 / NCAC, 1969 / *95*
Costumes / Joanne Ricca, assistant / NCAC, 1969 / *98*
Synchronizing / Joanne Ricca, assistant; Kathy Ahern, 16 / YBW, 1969 / *105*

*YBW = Yellow Ball Workshop
NCAC = Newton Creative Arts Center
PI = Projects Inc.
CDC = Cellar Door Cinema

Film Title / Student & Age / School* & Year / *Pages*

Charlie and His Harley / Mark Mahoney, 12 / NCAC, 1969 / *11*
Cinder City, "Smirk" / Peter Bull, 11 / CDC, 1966 / *13–15, 34†, 37*
The Country Scene / Andrea Dietrich, 11 / PI, 1966 / *26*
The Atomic Robot / Paul Falcone, 8 / CDC, 1967 / *26, 76†*
Eagle / Mimi Kravitz, 15 / NCAC, 1969 / *27*
The Bird Needs the Baby / Jean Falcone, 8 / YBW, 1969 / *29, 31*
The Idol / Billy Fuchs, 11 / NCAC, 1969 / *8, 33, 36*
Look Before You Leap / Michael DiGregorio, 14 / YBW, 1965 / *39*
Spectator / Steffen Pierce, 14 / CDC, 1967 / *39*
Smoke! Smoke! / Deirdre Cowden, 13 / CDC, 1966 / *49, 51†*
Move, Kid / Kathy Ahern, 16 / NCAC, 1969 / *53†, 63, 64–65†, 66–68*
The Park People / Group project / NCAC, 1967 / *54*
Underwater Creatures / Paul Falcone, 6 / YBW, 1965 / *56*
The Enlightenment / Mark Winer, 17; Larry Stern, 17 / NCAC, 1969 / *57, 58*
Just a Fishment of My Imagination / Carol Sones, 17 / NCAC, 1969 / *59*
The Yellow Submarine / Elsa Glassman, 16 / CDC, 1967 / *62*
$50,000 Per Fang / Steve DeTore, 13 / YBW, 1965 / *69*
Look Out! / Peter Finklestein, 12 / NCAC, 1968 / *82*
The Martians Are Coming / Paul Falcone, 10 / YBW, 1969 / *82*
The Hit / Anthony Schreiner, 12 / NCAC, 1968 / *83*
Fish / Yvonne Andersen / YBW, 1969 / *85†*
Eden / Amy Kravitz, 13 / NCAC, 1969 / *86, 88†, 89*
War Casualty / Amy Kravitz, 13 / NCAC, 1969 / *88†*
Krazy Times / Paul Falcone, 8; Jane Levy, 10; Susan Lenk, 10 / CDC, 1967 / *90*
Magic Mushroom / Karen Warschaurer, 14 / NCAC, 1969 / *92*
Shortcut / Rebecca Snider, 14 / NCAC, 1969 / *96*
Plague / Amy Schwartz, 15 / NCAC, 1969 / *97*
Coffin Child / Mark Winer, 17 / NCAC, 1969 / *98, 99*

† color picture

Index